'Knots tying
is easy ...

... and the more often you
practice it
the easier it becomes.'

Hazel Bailey – 1992

THE COMPLETE BOOK OF
SAILING
Knots

stoppers, bindings and shortenings
single, double and triple loops
bends
hitches
other useful knots

Geoffrey Budworth

The Lyons Press

First published in 2000 by Hamlyn
an imprint of Octopus Publishing Group Limited

All inquiries should be addressed to:
The Lyons Press,
123 West 18 Street,
New York, NY 10011

Library of Congress Cataloging In-Publication
data is available on file

ISBN 1-58574-067-5

Executive Editor Mike Evans
Commissioning Editor Nina Sharman
Editor Katey Day

Creative Director Keith Martin
Designer Mark Stevens
Illustration Line and Line

Production Controller Louise Hall

Photographic acknowledgements
Image Bank/Archive Photos 11 and 12
Octopus Publishing Group Ltd./Gary Latham 8–9 and 19
Tony Stone Images/Mark Segal 10

Typeset in Adobe Myriad, Monotype Walbaum and
Monotype Grotesque

Produced by Toppan Printing Co Ltd
Printed in China

contents

the knots

DIRECTORY OF KNOTS

<6>

<7>

ACKNOWLEDGEMENTS

I am indebted to Ron Prince and A.W. Trimm, of the 30th Bournemouth Sea Scouts, who in the early 1950s nurtured my innate liking for boats and cordage. They taught me my first knots and so began all that has happened to me since in the ropeworking world. I also recall here Jim Nicoll, ex-Shanghai detective and London river cop, who was my knot-tying mentor during the 1960s and 1970s; and I acknowledge those members of the International Guild of Knot Tyers* (too many to name without the risk of overlooking and omitting one, but they know who they are) who since 1982 have freely shared with me their expertise, and in doing so enlarged my own repertoire and understanding of knots. I also wish to thank James Martin, market coordinator at Marlow Ropes Ltd, for his time and help in updating me about yachting ropes, their construction, care and use.

* The superscript IGKT after a person's name in this book indicates that he or she is a member of the International Guild of Knot Tyers.

<8>

<9>

INTRODUCTION

> Upon acquiring his first boat the yachtsman discovers that its use is going to involve intimate personal contact with ropes and cordage.
>
> **Hervey Garrett Smith,** *The Arts of the Sailor* **(1953)**

This book is for all who go near boats of any kind – who gently punt, paddle, row, scull, sail or motor about quiet backwaters in kayaks, canoes and dinghies; or who hurtle, with split-second gymnastics (and almost unmanageable sail areas) around buoyed triangular race courses laid out on gravel pits and reservoirs, in tidal estuaries and offshore. It is also for those who cruise inland and coastal waters, and the saltwater sailors who venture out across deep and steeply heaving seas and oceans; for all who live or work aboard canal barges or narrowboats; and for those who play and sport on such diverse craft as white-water rafts, wet-bikes and jet-skis, hydrofoils or hovercraft, and powerboats. But even the casual land-bound observer who frequents marinas, quaysides, piers and causeways, or waterway locks will sooner or later be handed a rope's end by someone and expected to do something useful with it. Read on to learn what, how, where and when – and why.

<10>

HISTORY

Cordage and the first knots devised to make it work no doubt originated in prehistoric times for snaring and netting food, hauling and carrying loads – even for strangling those deemed to deserve it. Once a dug-out canoe or raft became too heavy to haul out of the water, however, some sort of anchor or mooring line was needed. One cannot simply park a floating boat and walk away: it must be tied up. Then, with the introduction of sail, all but the simplest masts required stays or shrouds to brace and support them, while even the crudest square-sail needed ropes to raise it, pull it in and let it out (trimming it to the wind), and this standing and running rigging grew in sophistication and complexity as boats evolved to cope with ever more venturesome journeys.

From river to estuary, sea to ocean, crews had to find stronger and more versatile knots to facilitate their boat-handling. Ferrymen, fishermen, smugglers and revenue officers; merchantmen and ships of war; voyages of exploration and discovery, conquest, trade, colonization and emigration – everyone who went afloat, for whatever reason, prior to the industrial revolution, had to know the ropes (literally) and that included lots of knots, too. Aboard the massive square-rigged sailing ships of the 18th century – such as the 1,000-ton cargo-cum-passenger ships of the English East India Company, His Majesty's 74-gun ships of the line, China tea clippers, windjammers laden with Australian wool, and the whaling fleets that pursued their quarry from the Arctic to the Antarctic – sailors' knots had become an art, a craft and a science.

To harness the wind that drove these leviathans, and made it possible to manoeuvre them, entailed masts and spars festooned with up to 30 miles of rope rigging weighing several imperial tons. As explained by American east-coast author Richard H. Dana (who went

<11>

polypropylene ousted vegetable-fibre ropes made from coir, cotton flax and hemp. It sometimes seems that there is little opportunity aboard a boat nowadays for tying knots.

Many previously essential knots are indeed redundant, due to the easy availability of thimbles, shackles and snap-hooks, jam and cam cleats, winches and mechanical line stoppers, rope clips, swaged fittings, turnbuckles, and a variety of other rigging terminals. Superb products – but, when wet and cold fingers drop the shackle pin overboard, the bit that remains is useless and might as well be tossed after it. And it is a fact of waterborne life that mechanical devices usually fail sea miles from a repair yard or chandlery that stocks a replacement, or at a time when such havens of help are closed and deserted. This is of particular concern to those on extended sea passages. Writer, historian and traveller Tim Severin, who in 1977 followed the trans-Atlantic route supposedly taken by the Irish monk St Brendan in the 7th century AD, summarized the problem in *The Brendan Voyage* (1978):

> Item by item, our modern equipment was collapsing under the conditions ... whenever a modern item broke, we tended to replace it with a home-made substitute devised from the ancient materials of wood, leather, and flax. These we could work and fashion, sew and shape to suit the occasion. The product usually looked cumbersome and rough, but it survived and we could repair it ourselves. Whereas when metal snapped, or plastic ripped, the only choice without a workshop on board was to jettison the broken item.

to sea as a common hand and worked his way around Cape Horn to California and back) in his book *Two Years Before the Mast* (1840), maintenance of the chafing gear alone aboard such a vessel was '... constant employment for a man or two men, during working hours, for a whole voyage.' Such ships were the biggest and most complicated moving mechanisms of which humankind was then capable, while the captains entrusted with these costly craft were the equivalent of astronauts, intrepid individuals able to take command of their massive (and often hard to handle) vessels, undertake the most hazardous of journeys into the unknown, and – more often than not – return with their command intact.

The advent of steam-powered and screw-driven iron ships, with wire rigging, anchor chains, and cranes to replace block-and-tackle hoists, eventually rendered all of this workaday commercial marlinespike rigging and seamanship obsolete. Knowledge of it lingered awhile in the rope-roughened hands of old sailormen, and was continued by rich yachtsmen and women with leisure and money to spend on classic boats and professional crews. Later, practitioners would include weekend sailing devotees and the blue water (or green water, or gunmetal gray water) single-handers and others who roamed the world in sailing boats. Until, that is, fibreglass and aluminium (aluminum) replaced painted wooden hulls and varnished spars, while synthetic monofilaments such as nylon, polyester and

Anyway, there ought to be a limit to how much cash is laid out on brand-name accessories, when a few metres (or yards) of line and the right combination of knots will work as well – and often better. For knots are

<12>

versatile; they can also be reused, weigh nothing and take up no space in locker or toolbox (knowledge of them being stored in one's head and hands). Regular use of knots in preference to a pricey clip, clamp or other gadget could also prove eco-friendly, if the practice ultimately compelled manufacturers to reduce unneeded output and so moderated consumption of the planet's scarce and finite energy sources.

Although so many boating knots have pedigrees that can be traced back to the epoch of square-rigged sailing ships, it is a mistake to adhere slavishly to dated seamanship and rigging manuals and the later knot books based upon them. Synthetic rope and cordage differ greatly from the fibrous hawsers and cables that those knots were devised to hold. Some classic knots perform less well in modern lines; others, distrusted by old-time sailormen, are now regarded favourably. The knotting scene, far from being fossilized or moribund, is a lively one that is still evolving. New knots are discovered and reported every year. It is true that the days are gone when dockyard riggers and sailormen – 'every finger a marlinespike,

every hair a rope's yarn' (never really true) – devised and named new knots, bends and hitches. Today it is anglers and climbers (on mountains, in caves, surveying civil-engineering structures or in hostile assault situations) who are the innovative knot tyers. The properties demanded of any knot by these two disparate groups are similar, since both require knots that are strong and secure – only the scale differs. Climbing knots are tied in sheath-and-core ropes, cords and tape (webbing) with cross-sections hundreds of times larger than angling monofilaments and breaking strengths thousands of times greater. Anglers are concerned only to preserve costly tackle and catch that elusive prize-winning or record-breaking fish. Their jamming knots (which must be cut off afterwards) are not matters of life or death – at least not to the human manipulating the rod and line. A climber's life hangs upon the knots he or she chooses to use, yet must be undone again without undue damage to the ropes in which they are tied. It follows that some climbing knots are suitable for use aboard boats, and a few will be included in the sections that follow.

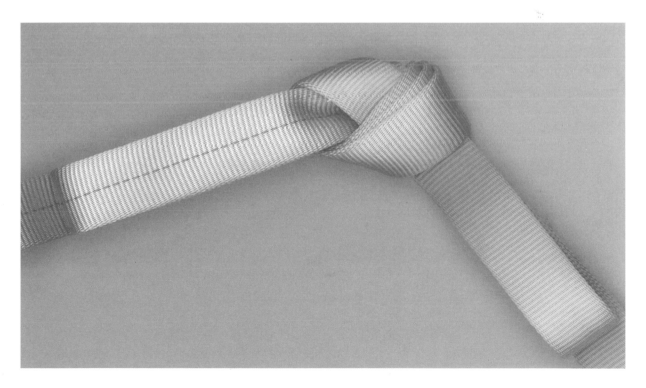

<13>

terms, tips and techniques

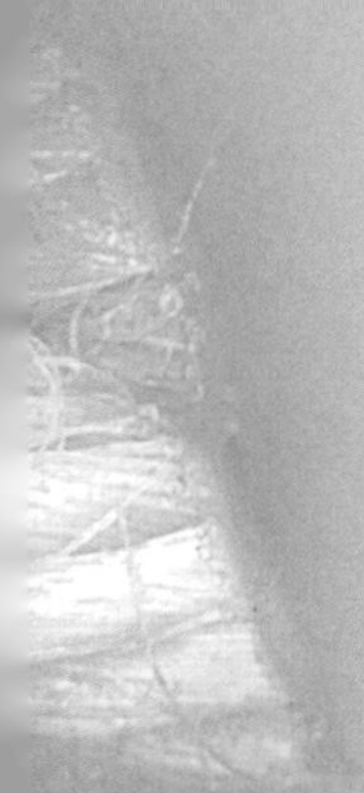

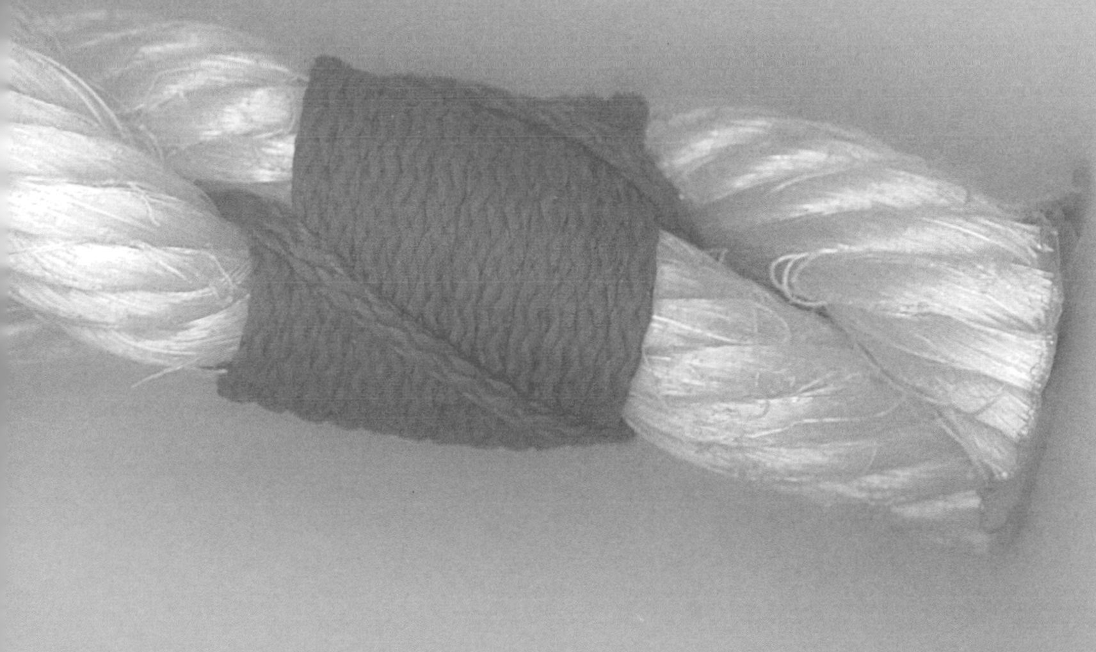

USEFUL TERMS

So my first piece of advice about rope on a boat is: have plenty of it, in assorted kinds and sizes.

Roger C. Taylor, *Knowing the Ropes* (1989)

Fluency in sea and freshwater boating jargon is an essential prerequisite, and some of the terms have to do with ropes and knots.

A rope or cord has two ends; the one used to tie a knot is the working end and the inert one is the standing end (fig.1). Between these two extremities lies the standing part of the rope. A bend that forms a U-shape (more or less) is a bight, while a bight with a crossing point becomes a loop. Twist a loop just once more and linked elbows result. Passing a rope over a bollard or around a towing post, for whatever purpose, is known as taking a turn; and, when the working end is carried further around to join its own standing part (often preparatory to tucking and tying), this becomes a round turn (fig. 2).

A three-strand rope is a hawser-laid rope or simply a hawser; three such hawsers laid up together left-handed create a cable-laid rope or just a cable

(seen infrequently, now that a single synthetic hawser is so very strong). Rope that is stiff, owing to its tight construction, is said to be hard-laid, while a looser structure that is more flexible is soft-laid. Any lesser cordage is informally referred to as small stuff. Domestic small stuff is familiarly known as string, while fine lines of better quality are distinguished as twine or thread.

Ropes in use are referred to as lines (bow line, breast line, stern line, lifeline, heaving line, towline). A line secured to the stern of a boat and used to moor it to a quay, dockside, jetty or buoy, or for making it fast to another vessel, is a painter; and any bit of rope less than about 9m (30ft) long, casually used as a makeshift mooring attachment, is a lazy painter. Mooring lines arranged to prevent a boat surging forward or back in its berth (or to swing it around, either by hand or engine, using a combination of rope and tide) are known as springs. A short length of cord used to lash or secure an item of equipment, and often tied around a person's neck, wrist or waist to prevent a knife or other tool from being lost overboard or dropped on to the deck while working aloft, is a lanyard.

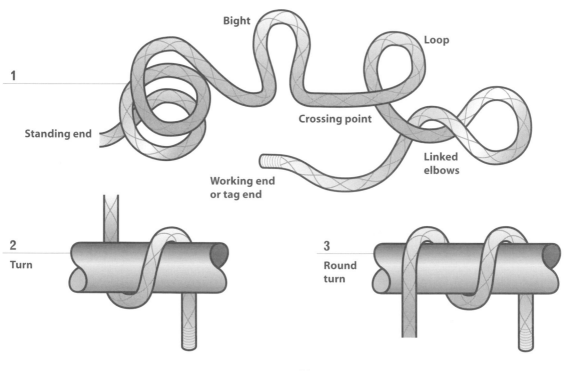

<16>

TOOLS

Almost all of the knots, seizings and whippings in this book can be tied with hands and fingers, unaided by a single tool. A few knots, especially if tied in small stuff, are best tightened with tools; and tight knots may then need an implement to loosen them again. Treatment of ropes' ends, to prevent fraying, can also require a few accessories. The following basic toolkit is adequate for those needs.

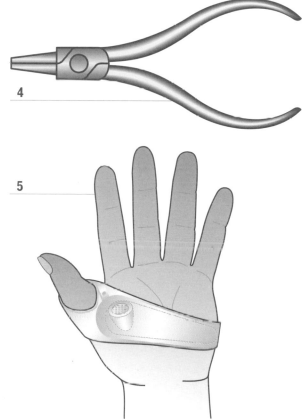

Everyone who goes afloat should carry a **sailor's knife** (fig. 1) – preferably a sheath knife (which is stronger), although a folding pocket knife is sometimes more convenient. It should have a straight edge (kept sharp) with little or no point. The handle should be contoured for a firm, slip-resistant grip, with a hole through which a lanyard is attached.

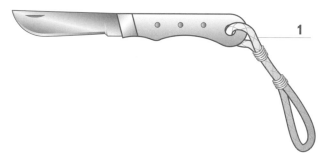

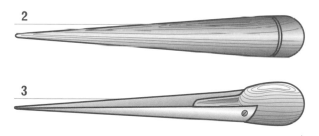

Fids (fig. 2) are hardwood spikes, intended principally for parting the strands of traditional ropes to splice them, but they can also be indispensable for poking and prising apart tight knots so as to untie them. They are available in many different sizes, but 22cm (8–9in) is a useful all-purpose length.

The modern stainless-steel development of the wooden fid, the **Swedish fid** (fig. 3), is preferable; when forced between two strands that are reluctant to separate, its hollow cross-section retains a space through which another cord or strand may then be inserted. The name dates back to at least the 1960s, when the original product was stamped 'Made in Sweden'.

Pliers (fig. 4) that have jaws with gripping surfaces filed smooth are best, and round-billed ones best of all, so as to avoid damaging individual fibres or monofilaments when tugging at strands and knot parts.

A sailmaker's palm (fig. 5) is a leather strap designed to go around the human hand and is fitted with a reinforced and dimpled metal mount. It is the sailor's equivalent of a household thimble, employed to force thick sewing needles and twine through canvas and rope with the heel of the hand. Necessarily robust

to protect the user from accidental self-inflicted stab wounds, the best makes are also flexible enough not to chafe the wearer, and adjustable to size by means of a small buckle at the back. Left-handed versions, as illustrated, are available as well as right-handed.

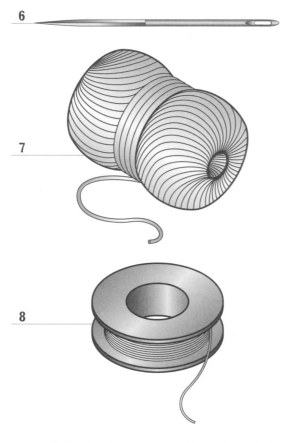

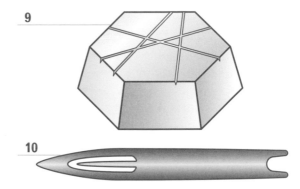

pulled across its upper surface (creating a criss-cross of shallow grooves) to weather-proof them. Doubled threads treated this way are easier to use as they tend to cling together after waxing.

Netting needles (fig. 10) are hand-held bobbins primarily intended for net-making, and are ideal for storing quantities of small cords and twines tangle-free (suppliers will demonstrate how to load them). Made of plastic, wood or metal, they can be bought (or home-made) in a variety of sizes from 11.5cm (4¾in) to 30cm (1ft) or more in length.

Even non-smokers will find it worthwhile to arm themselves with a butane-fuelled flame source – a **cigarette lighter** (fig. 11) – for a quick way to heat-seal the ends of cut cordage.

Adhesive tape (fig. 12) is handy for taping the ends of ropes prior to more thorough treatment with whipping twine.

Sailmaker's needles (fig. 6) are triangular in cross-section. Each size has a number, #1 being the largest. For stitched whippings, #12, #14 or #16 are about right, depending upon the size of the ropework in hand.

Spunyarn (fig. 7) is for the ends of larger ropes, **whipping twine** (fig. 8) for lesser diameters. Nylon or Terylene (Dacron) is stronger and lasts longer than natural fibre. It may come already waxed and weather-proofed by the manufacturer.

Beeswax (fig. 9) is an amber resinous compound, sold in small blocks, with its own mild but distinctive smell. Whipping and sewing twines are

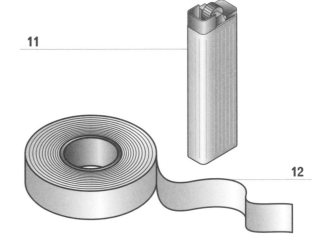

CORDAGE MATERIALS

All rope and other cordage for boating was once made from the shredded fibres of plant leaves (sisal, manila), seeds (cotton) and stems (flax, hemp, jute), and from other curious sources such as coir from the husks of coconuts. These vegetable-fibre ropes – white cotton excepted – were attractive shades of blonde or brunette, and darker if impregnated with tar for weather-proofing, with not unpleasant smells evocative of the distant lands in which their raw materials had originally grown. Their artful geometry was a tribute to the craft of the ropemaker. People enchanted by the lure and lore of sailing ships, who wish that such vessels still ornamented the skyline with their Euclidian silhouettes, regret the demise of vegetable-fibre ropes; others, worried by humankind's commitment to ecological despoliation, hope for a partial return to biodegradable natural-fibre cordage, made from renewable growing crops. Indeed, natural-fibre cordage can still be obtained, often at a premium price that reflects its change in status, to re-rig and equip classic wooden boats with hempen rigging, tarred spunyarn seizings and fenders of water-resistant coir. It can also be seen in the décor of nautical pubs, sailing club-houses and seaside restaurants.

But natural-fibre rope was always hard on the hands and, by today's standards, weak. It was somewhat stronger when wet, but then swelled so that knots tied in it were liable to jam and became impossible to untie. It was prone to rot and mildew, unless painstakingly dried before storage – then it was vulnerable to attack by insects and vermin. Greater strength could only be achieved by using large and increasingly unmanageable circumferences; the anchor cables of hemp aboard a 100-gun British warship of 1805 were 60cm (24in) in circumference (18cm/7½in in diameter). Natural-fibre ropes were quickly damaged by abrasion, and in wet and icy conditions they froze – when further use caused the brittle fibres to snap, irreparably weakening the affected strands. With the emergence of synthetic materials, these shortcomings became intolerable.

Nylon was the first of the synthetic fibres to become commercially available for ropemaking, although at first it was an expensive product that only

<19>

a limited number of customers could afford. There are two grades of nylon: nylon 66 was discovered in the Du Pont laboratories, followed by nylon 6 which was developed by I.G. Farbenindustrie. Next came polyester fibre, marketed in the UK as Terylene (and elsewhere as Dacron). This was a British development, from investigations at the Calico Printers Association, the sole rights of which were taken up by Imperial Chemical Industries. Then, in the late 1950s, the simpler hydrocarbon ethylene was incorporated into a ropemaking fibre; polyethylene (polythene) was a cheaper product than either nylon or Terylene and, although the ropes made from it were not as strong as those made from nylon, it was still superior to the traditional hard-fibre yarns – and the first synthetic rope to float.

The major breakthrough in synthetic fibres, however, was the discovery that polypropylene could be polymerized (made into long molecular chains) to create a rope yarn of high tenacity. Polypropylene was ideal for extrusion on low-cost machines and produced a fibre considerably stronger and even lighter than polyethylene. The raw material was a by-product of the oil industry and consequently very cheap, so that synthetic fibre could now compete with sisal and even

manila on almost equal terms. Polypropylene quickly became available in a variety of forms ranging from filaments to films, which could be twisted into rope yarns. These products were – and remain – the big four 'Ps' of ropemaking, namely: polyamide (nylon); polyester (Terylene or Dacron); polyethylene (polythene); and polypropylene.

The smoother surface of these new-fangled synthetics, which rendered some knots, bends and hitches less secure, was troublesome in the early days. I recall in the mid-1960s the first time I belayed a shiny white polypropylene mooring rope – to a cleat on the quarter of a police duty motorboat – with a quick turn, a figure-of-eight, and another (unsecured) turn. Then I watched it slowly unwrap itself. An old tug master told me that his reflexes were all wrong for nylon towing lines; whenever he gave a touch ahead to pull the bow or stern of a ship around, he was failing to allow enough time to take up the amazing amount of stretch inherent in a nylon rope before the towed vessel began to react – then, unless he stopped pulling sooner than seemed right to him, the elastic recoil imparted too much swing. And a lighterman had his hand sliced open to the tendons by the ragged heat-sealed and hardened end of a hawser that was pulled through his

<20>

grasp by a maverick 100-ton laden barge.

Despite old seadogs and river workers being compelled to learn new tricks for new ropes, within a decade synthetic cordage had almost entirely replaced natural-fibre ropes aboard boats. Up to 95 per cent of all yachting ropes are now nylon or polyester, with the remaining 5 per cent accounted for by polypropylene and the so-called 'miracle fibres' (Kevlar, and Dyneema or Spectra).

POLYAMIDE (NYLON)

Nylon is the strongest synthetic cordage (although 10–15 per cent weaker when wet) and is cheaper than polyester. It is very elastic, being able to stretch under a severe load by an average of 25 per cent, and then regain its original length when the load is removed. This makes it suitable for mooring and towing lines, and it is widely used in the offshore oil industry in those roles. As it does not float, nylon can also be used for anchor warps or ropes. Buy white, as colouring can weaken the fibres by up to 10 per cent (as well as add to the price). A fairly high melting point of around 260°C (500°F) means a reduced risk of failure due to friction, but be warned – like all synthetic fibres, it will soften, glaze and be permanently weakened at a much lower temperature than its actual melting point. Nylon ropes withstand attack from alkalis (and acids to a lesser degree), oils and organic solvents. They resist photochemical degradation from the ultraviolet (UV) wavelengths in sunlight fairly well. Resistance to damage by abrasion is good when the cordage is slack, less good when it is loaded (so protect vulnerable sections from chafe). It can be stored wet or dry.

POLYESTER (BRAND NAMES TERYLENE OR DACRON)

Terylene® (UK) or Dacron® (US) is almost as strong as nylon and weakens scarcely at all when wet. It is about 15 per cent heavier, with little elasticity, and much of that is often removed by pre-stretching during manufacture. This combination of high tensile strength and low elasticity makes it ideal for standing rigging,

<21>

halyards and sheets. Polyester has about the same melting point as nylon and similar resistance to chemical attack, but is noticeably tougher where photochemical deterioration, acids and chafe are involved. Like nylon, it does not float and may be stored wet or dry.

POLYPROPYLENE

In terms of cost and performance, polypropylene can be ranked between vegetable fibre and the superior synthetics (nylon and Terylene or Dacron). It is a thermoplastic which melts at lower temperatures (120–180°C/250–350°F) and has a density about 10 per cent lower than water – so it floats. One-third less strong than dry nylon, it has about the same resistance to stretch as Terylene or Dacron, but is much more vulnerable to chafe and chemical degradation (including UV damage from sunlight). Limit its use to deck lashings, clothes lines, flag halyards, fender lanyards, dinghy painters, lifelines and heaving lines. There is a three-strand polypropylene rope resembling hemp that would not look amiss on classic wooden boats, as long as its weaker performance is borne in mind.

'MIRACLE FIBRES'

Kevlar – discovered by Du Pont as long ago as 1965 – is an organic polymer immune to moisture and rot. Weight-for-weight it is twice as strong as nylon; with less stretch than Terylene or Dacron, it has even been used to replace wire halyards. It is, however, very brittle (bending and flexing can result in self-inflicted lacerations).

Then there is Dyneema® from the Far East, and its American counterpart HMPE (high modulus polyethylene) or Spectra® (the brand name of Allied Chemicals, who began manufacturing this super-lightweight polyethylene in 1986). Its phenomenal tensile strength is greater than that of stainless steel, and it is more tolerant of flexing than Kevlar, which it looks set to supersede. The considerable cost and limitations of these state-of-the-art products will not deter experimental racing sailors, for whom competitive edge and extra safety margins are worth any price, but they are not recommended for routine knot tying.

<22>

CORDAGE CONSTRUCTION

The mechanized process of making a hawser-laid rope begins by spinning selected natural fibres or synthetic monofilaments into long yarns, which spiral right-handed or clockwise. A bundle of yarns is then twisted left-handed or anti-/counter-clockwise to form a strand. Then three of these strands are laid right-handed (clockwise) to create the actual rope (fig. 1). Some knot tyers refer to a right-handed lay as Z-laid, and a left-handed lay as S-laid, but these terms come from textile craftworkers and are heard much less aboard boats. It is this twist and counter-twist which provides the adhesion, enabling a hawser-laid rope to retain its characteristic form and function. Consequently, if three hawsers are used to make a cable, they must helix left-handed (anti-/counter-clockwise); and, since each hawser is composed of three strands, a cable will inevitably have nine strands. Another way to make giant ropes – say for supertankers – is to plait them with four pairs of strands (fig. 2), and any anchor warp or rope made like this is easier to attach to a length of ground tackle chain.

Natural-fibre cordage was rarely braided (except for flag halyards and patent log-lines). Most synthetic rope and smaller stuff is, however, a sheath of either eight or sixteen parts plaited around a core made up of hundreds of filaments. This heart may be arranged simply as parallel yarns (fig. 3), hawser-laid (fig. 4), or plaited (fig. 5). Some plaited cores are themselves hollow and require heart strands to fill them; the result is then a trio of concentric layers – an outer sheath, an inner sheath and a core (fig. 6). In all these sheath-and-core or braid-on-braid constructions, it is usual for each component to perform a discrete function. For example, a dock line may consist of a nylon core (which allows elongation to prevent shock loads being transmitted to cleats and other hardware), with an extensible braided cover of polyester to resist abrasion. For sheets aboard cruising yachts, a three-strand core of polyester provides strength and durability, while a sixteen-plait matt cover is comfortable to handle.

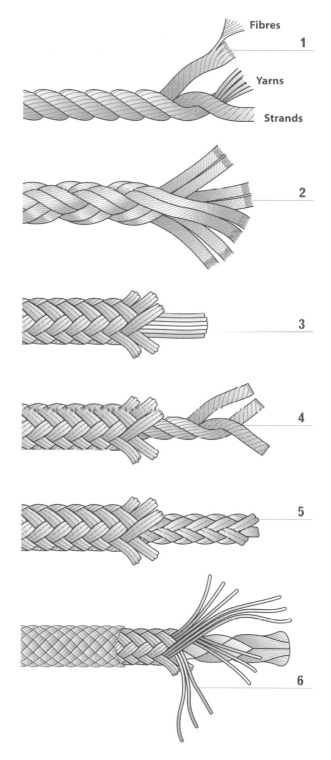

Fibres
1

Yarns

Strands

2

3

4

5

6

A monofilament is more than 50 microns ($^1/_{500}$in) in diameter and of uniform circular cross-section along its length. Exceptionally low stretch – say, for dinghy spinnaker sheets and control lines – is achieved by means of polyester multifilaments, which are very fine continuous clusters of filaments, each of which is less than 50 microns ($^1/_{500}$in) but again of uniform diameter and circular cross-section along its length. It is because monofilaments and multifilaments run the length of the cordage that greater strength and a smoother finish result – but this, at the same time, can also make knots less secure.

It is the fact that natural fibres can only be as long as the leaf or stalk from which they came that ultimately limits the strength of the hawser or cable containing them, and it is the countless number of fibre ends emerging on the surface that also accounts for the rough texture and friction of these ropes. As some users find this a desirable handling characteristic, most manufacturers provide at least one synthetic product that recreates it, by chopping polypropylene monofilaments or multifilaments into staple fibre lengths from as little as 2cm ($^3/_4$in) up to 2m (2yd), then spinning and laying them up into hairy hawsers.

Man-made cordage comes in various solid colours, or with contrasting marker yarns creating spiral flecks and patterns, so that it is now feasible to colour-code yacht halyards and sheets; or one may simply follow (or set) the latest trend in rigging a dinghy, kayak or sailboard.

Pre-metric knot books referred to the size of any rope by its circumference in inches, so a rope referred to as 1$^1/_2$in was actually less than $^1/_2$in thick. Nowadays all cordage is more realistically known by its diameter in centimetres (or millimetres), converting that same 1$^1/_2$in rope to 12mm. Anything over 10mm diameter is traditionally a rope, but as synthetic cordage is so much stronger than natural fibre, common sense dictates that some lines with smaller diameters must also be ropes. For example, the mainsheet for a 10m (33ft) yacht may be only 8mm diameter, yet the average breaking load of even a dinghy sheet of eight-plait polypropylene that size is over 0.5 tonne; a sheath-and-core (three-strand) polyester halyard tail or sheet of polyester aboard something larger would be nearer 2 tonnes; and a similar-diameter racing yacht line in Spectra/Dyneema almost 3 tonnes.

Lines less than 6mm diameter are not recommended for halyards and sheets, as they can be difficult to hold and uncomfortable to pull. Nothing much above 30mm diameter should normally be needed for any non-industrial purpose afloat; a 32mm multi-plait nylon anchor warp has a breaking strength of nearly 24 tonnes.

<24>

CARE OF ROPE AND CORDAGE

Ropes and other cordage are dynamic, high-tech and expensive products, so it makes sense to take care of them. Wear and tear occurs during normal handling and usage. This is inevitable but should be minimized to preserve reliability, durability and performance.

• Protect sections of line against predictable chafe by means of leather sleeves, rubber or plastic tubing, foam pipe insulation, tape or spunyarn. Ratchets and stoppers are particularly hard on the outer surface of ropes. Obvious signs of wear will occur if ropes remain in the same position for long periods of use, when thought should be given to reversing them (end for end) in order to vary and spread the load. Alternatively, a slightly longer rope might be used in the first place, then periodically shifted a few centimetres (or inches) to change the points of chafe. Blocks, cleats and fairleads should be of a size that allows the rope to pass freely through and around them to minimize the risk of abrasion. Be alert to prevent or rectify seized-up blocks and swivels.

• Inspect ropes frequently for wear and weakness. When handling them, routinely look for tell-tale signs of deterioration and determine what future action is required. Some surface hairiness is no bad thing in an otherwise well-cared-for rope. While it may imply a slight loss of strength due to broken surface fibres, the fuzziness helps to protect the rope from further abrasion. Extensive areas of broken outer fibres, however, are a warning sign that the rope may soon have to be replaced. Hawser-laid lines should also be grasped in both hands and gently twisted here and there, to open the three strands and gain a glimpse of the rope's inner condition.

• The possibility of a rope failing completely due to friction-generated heat reaching melting point is unlikely, but localized glazing (fusing of adjacent fibres and yarns that have been subjected to fierce friction) may occur. Extensive glazing impairs a rope's performance.

• Since the innards of any sheath-and-core line lie concealed within the outer braid, only gross flaws or failings (such as a bulging rupture through a torn sheath) will show. A sheath that creeps over its inner core, due to differing degrees of elasticity, is also indicative of cordage construction that is somehow failing. Other than that, the inner condition of sheath-and-core ropes can only be surmised from their history. A log book for each halyard, sheet, mooring and anchor warp would be ideal; the alternative is personal knowledge of a rope's age, together with the use, misuse and abuse to which it has been subjected, after which shrewd judgement must dictate when it should be retired from active service.

• Do not throw a rope carelessly down on to a rough surface or drag it along beach or dockside. Avoid stepping on ropes needlessly.

• Even lack of use – oddly enough – ages ropes. It is a mistake to assume that one purchased new and then for some reason not used for a year or two will still be in absolutely prime condition.

• At least once a year, hose down lines in fresh water or machine wash them (in a mesh bag to prevent bad tangles) using a mild soap, to flush out sea-salt crystals, sand and other grit. Dry them in fresh air and stow away from sunlight.

• It has been said that stiff new line, which is not always amenable or nice to handle, is probably at its best; once it softens and becomes a pleasure to work with, watch out – it is deteriorating fast. Suspect ropes must be downgraded from tasks where failure would be dangerous or costly to less crucial work, and lines not fit for any duty afloat should be condemned and discarded altogether (except, perhaps, for learning and practising knots on shore).

TECHNIQUES

COILING

In the open fields or gloomy sheds where cordage products were once made, a rope could only be the length of the ropewalk – perhaps 30m (33yd), at most 0.5km (⅓ mile) – although two or more such ropes could then be spliced together. Now, with compact modern machinery, they can be any length the customer requires. To handle and store even a comparatively short 30m (98ft) length of rope, however, it must be coiled.

Coiling has to take into account the inherent tendency of rope to twist and form unwanted figure-of-eight loops which, if impatiently pulled, insert themselves one inside another to convert what was an orderly coil into an absolute bird's nest of a tangle. Worse, one or more loops may be forced into small, hard kinks – like varicose veins – that permanently disfigure and weaken the rope. And a coil carefully done and laid to rest in the depths of a locker or car boot (trunk) can, when retrieved, still emerge with all this mischief present, even after minimal handling. As the character Carruthers reported in Erskine Childers' novel *The Riddle of the Sands* (1938):'I wrestled with intractable ropes, slaves if they could be subdued, tyrants if they got the upper hand.'

A coil offers some hope of making rope behave, whether it is to keep working lines from under the feet of active crews, or for long-term storage. Afloat or alongside, experienced sailors habitually pick up, coil and place out of harm's way straying lengths of line, while with most of their minds they consider other boating needs – in much the same way that snooker players chalk their cues whenever they survey the disposition of the balls on the table.

The basic rule is to coil right-handed ropes clockwise (that is, right-handed). At the same time a right-hand (clockwise) roll or twist must be imparted to the rope itself, with the wrist of the coiling hand, each time a circular turn is made and placed alongside the preceding turns. If these twists were not inserted, extremely hard-laid ropes might actually coil up into a series of figures-of-eight. What generally occurs, however, is that each coiled turn has a slight twist that prevents it from lying flat. Uncorrected, these partial imperfections would accumulate to create the sort of unusable tangle already described, so twist is deliberately put in during coiling to tame each turn. But this means that when the rope is run out again, it will retain those twists. The reason for coiling right-handed ropes clockwise is so that when the rope is uncoiled, the right-hand lay can unlay itself slightly to relieve the tension. It may still be preferable – if time and space allow – to uncoil the rope completely and then shake it systematically from the working end towards an unattached standing end, to remove the residual twists. Natural-fibre ropes, new from the manufacturer, can retain such an imprint of the coils in which they were delivered that I have seen them towed astern for several hours to erase that memory and straighten them out.

Left-handed rope – something of a rarity – should be coiled anti-/counter-clockwise for the reasons outlined above. Braided lines might, therefore, go either way, but so ingrained does the habit of coiling right-handed become that there is a tendency to keep to the orthodox practice and coil these right-handed, too.

<26>

There is a choice of coiling methods, subdivided into two broad categories: halyards, sheets and mooring-line coils must be suspended tidily but ready for instant use, whereas ropes to be conveyed and stored can (and ought to) be more securely tied to keep them in order.

Method 1 – 'stops', etc.

Manufacturers sell and deliver rope wound by machine into compact coils, held together with several short lengths of spunyarn known as 'stops' (fig. 1). Cut these off and re-coil the purchase more loosely, replacing the discarded stops with another temporary securing device, such as a couple of strangle knots with draw-loops (figs 2–3).

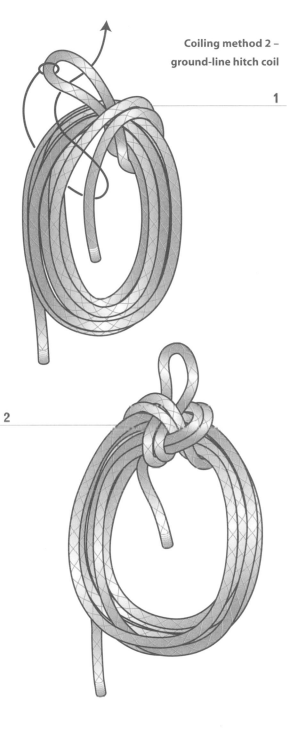

**Coiling method 2 –
ground-line hitch coil**

1

2

**Coiling method 1 –
'stops'**

1

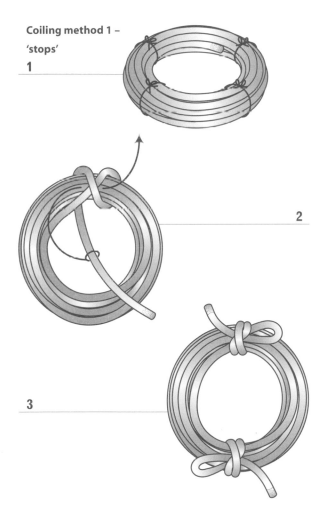

2

3

Method 2 – ground-line hitch coil

This is another storage coil. With a doubled working end, tie a ground-line hitch around the top of the coil (figs 1–2).

<27>

Coiling method 3 – Alpine coil

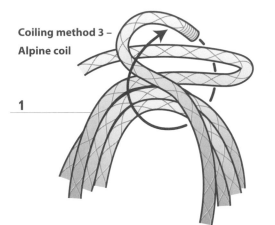

1

2

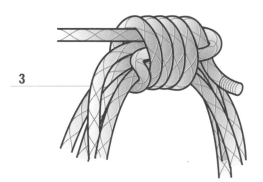

3

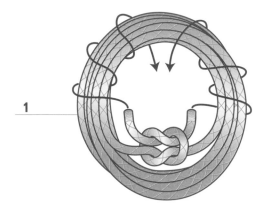

1

Coiling method 4 – wrapped and reef-knotted coil

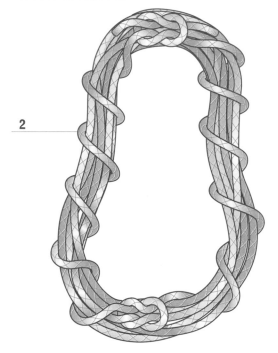

2

Method 3 – Alpine coil

To carry a coil over your shoulder, bring both ends to the top of the newly made coil and form a bight in one of them (fig. 1). Wrap the other end as shown and tuck it through the bight first formed (fig. 2). Pull on the bight to close it and so trap the end (fig. 3).

Method 4 – wrapped and reef-knotted coil

This is the way to convey a coil together with other kit in the boot (trunk) of a car, or stuffed inside a sail bag, with a reasonable expectation that it will emerge at the end of its journey in the same state that it started. Bring the two ends together at the bottom of the coil and tie them with a reef (square) knot (fig. 1). Wrap each long end around and up an adjacent leg of the coil until these two working ends meet at the top, where they are again reef knotted (fig. 2).

<28>

Method 5 – figure-of-eight coil

This method is used to hang a rope from a locker hook or mast cleat. The name refers to the method of securing it, not to the way it is coiled – although that too is unorthodox, done as it is with the rope first doubled. Then coil it (fig. 1), wrap the bight as shown (fig. 2) and finally tuck it up through the top of the coil (fig. 3).

Method 6 – buntline or gasket coil

Use this method to coil and hank a working line when anchored, moored or berthed (docked) with sails furled – for instance, to hang the main sheet from the boom. First wrap the working end several times to enclose both legs of the coil (figs 1–2). Then pull a bight through, as shown (fig. 3), and fit it down over the coil to lie snugly alongside the earlier turns (figs 4–5).

Coiling method 6 – buntline or gasket coil

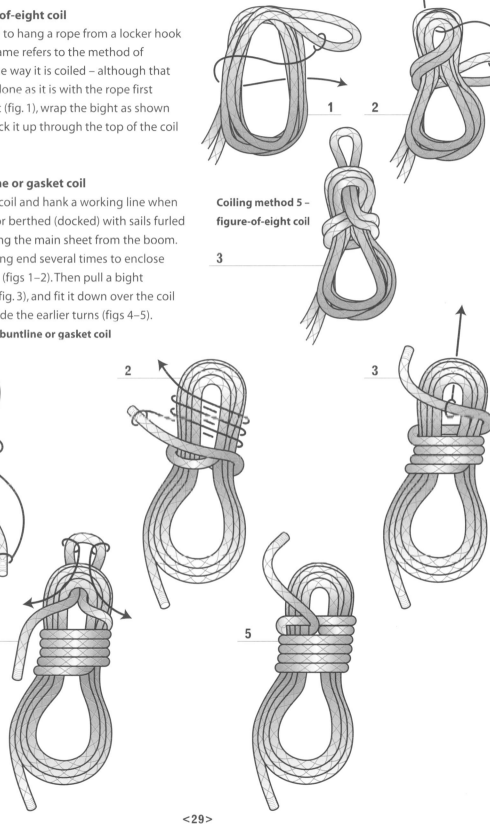

Coiling method 5 – figure-of-eight coil

<29>

Method 7 – halyard coil

To keep halyard falls or tails out of harm's way, having first belayed around a cleat or pin, coil the remainder of the halyard and twist a bight as shown (fig. 1). Loop that bight up and around to contain the coil and hold it on the cleat or pin, from which it can be readily cast off preparatory to altering sail (fig. 2).

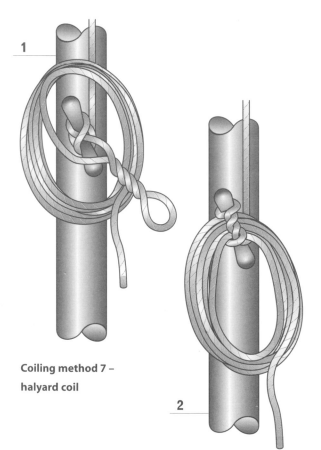

Coiling method 7 – halyard coil

It is possible to coil in a succession of figures-of-eight (not illustrated); and, as no twist needs to be imparted during coiling, lines coiled this way can be run out again without twisting or snagging; but such coils are not so handily made or stored. So, although an awareness of sound coiling technique is essential so as to handle rope effectively, there is no need to make too much of it. After all, a light heaving line is coiled readily enough and – when thrown from practised hands – uncoils itself satisfactorily.

FLAKING

Flaking (or cheesing) down a line is not a practical alternative to coiling, but rather the ornamental display of a spare rope, aboard posh yachts and public-sector craft used to convey senior officers and VIPs.

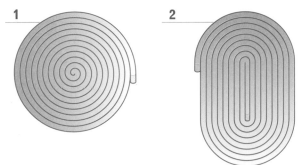

A Flemish flake is one flat spiral layer which is generally circular (fig. 1). Ropes may be coiled down, from the middle outwards, with some two-handed patting and pressing to ensure neatness as the work progresses, but there is a more lubberly approach that works better. Starting from the middle, turn the growing flake anti-/counter-clockwise like a wheel. If the end refuses to lie close to the body of the flake, stop it with a length of twine or spunyarn. An elliptical flake (fig.2) can be made to squeeze into a narrow space.

A French flake is one built up into three or four layers by working alternately from the inside out, then outside in, with each succeeding layer one turn smaller than the one upon which it rests (figs 3–4).

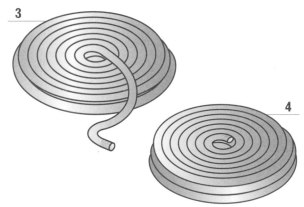

<30>

At Waterloo Pier, an operational Metropolitan Police station that rose and fell with the Thames tide in central London, the chief inspector's launch crew that I knew in the 1960s always displayed a spare 18m (60ft) salvage line flaked down on top of the stern locker. It was made in the form of a long and loose ellipse, the middle of which was then pulled over itself (fig. 5) to create an unusual triple-eyed effect.

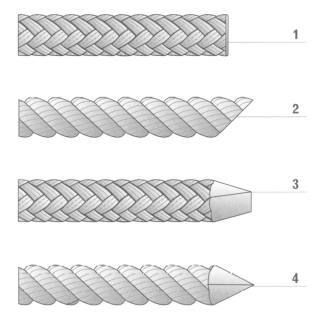

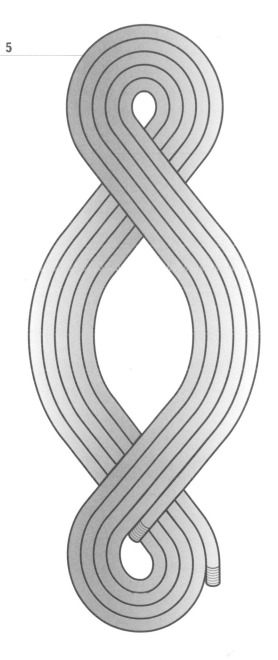

HEAT-SEALING

Rope manufacturers and stockists melt, cut and seal the synthetic ropes and cords they sell with an electrically heated guillotine blade. Because this is a costly piece of equipment, heavy for its size, dependent upon a power source – and with no other useful function – most of us make do with cheap alternatives.

The cool yellow flame from a match or cigarette lighter is adequate for small stuff, but a soldering iron with the appropriate blade makes a neater finish. For ropes and large cordage, heat (and reheat at frequent intervals) an old knife blade in the hot blue flame of a butane/propane DIY blowtorch, until it glows cherry-red. The handle of the knife must be of wood or some other material that does not conduct heat. Do not try to cut or saw; let the heat do the work. The heat-sealed end may be straight (fig. 1), slanted (fig. 2), chiselled (fig. 3), or bevelled (fig. 4). Resist the temptation to touch the work with inquisitive fingers, as melted gobs of synthetic cordage can adhere to, blister and burn the skin. For small stuff, heat-sealing may be all that is required. Larger work ought to be whipped, but heat-sealing, tying or taping is an acceptable first aid treatment.

<31>

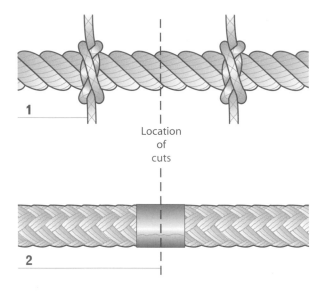

1

Location
of
cuts

2

TYING AND TAPING

A binding knot is an acceptable alternative to heat-sealing a rope's end, and – especially if two of the knots are placed side by side – is likely to last as long. Before cutting a rope, always apply a strangle or constrictor knot on either side of the place where you intend to cut it (fig. 1).

Wrapping two or three turns of adhesive tape around the end of a rope is an unattractive substitute for a twine whipping, but doubtless the old timers would have done it if they could. It is still better than doing nothing, and some tapes have a look about them (texture or colour) that is not so unsightly. To prepare a rope prior to cutting it, even when it is to be whipped, apply a broad tape and then simply slice it in half (fig. 2), to secure both ends at a single stroke. To cut rope or cordage with a knife, if hand-strength is insufficient, tap or pound the back of the blade with a wooden mallet or something else as hefty.

SLEEVES AND ADHESIVES

Some chandlers supply plastic tubing which, cut into short sleeves, can be fitted over a rope's end and then heated (for example, by holding over a steaming kettle), to shrink it and form an artificial whipping that way. There is also a brand of liquid whipping, into which you dip the rope's end and then withdraw it and allow to dry; or, for small stuff, simply cover any cut end with one of the many latex-based or polyvinyl acetate adhesives, and let it congeal.

WHIPPING

A frayed line is not only troublesome to use, it is – considering the price per metre (or yard) of marine cordage – a costly waste. Never cut a rope or cord without first ensuring that both severed ends have been prevented by one method or another from fraying; and deal promptly with any rope's end that sheds its whipping or other seizing (tape or twine).

Whipping is the name given to the process of wrapping and tightly seizing a rope's end with relatively thin but strong waxed twine, spunyarn or cord (depending upon the diameter of the rope). For clarity, the step-by-step illustrations in this book show a much thicker line than should actually be used. Bind synthetic ropes with synthetic twine, and use natural-fibre twine on ropes of vegetable origin. Since whippings must be tightly applied, a twine that breaks during the tying process is too weak and should be swapped for stronger stuff.

When only the strands of a neglected hawser-laid rope's end have separated, it may be possible to lay

<32>

them back up again. Give each strand a strong left-handed (anti-/counter-clockwise) twist as it is re-laid right-handed (clockwise) into the groove between the other two strands, so as to regenerate the alternate twist and counter-twist that will enable them to cling together once more. The result is unlikely to look like new again, as human hands do not generate the power and precision of the original machine lay. Then tie or tape as already described, prior to whipping.

Once the strands themselves have frayed, which occurs almost instantaneously when hard-laid synthetic lines are cut or lose their whippings, it is impossible to re-lay the rope. In this case, tie or tape at least 2.5cm (1in) back from where the fraying begins. Always whip intact rope, then cut off the spoilt stuff.

Method 1 – common whipping
This is the least secure of whippings, adequate only for ropes not subjected to heavy use. Lay a bight of twine along the body of the rope and bind the working end around for a distance at least equivalent to the rope's diameter (fig. 1). Tuck the working end through what remains of the loop and pull the standing end until the loop disappears beneath the wrapping turns (fig. 2), taking the working end with it. Stop pulling when the resulting two interlocked elbows are in the centre of the whipping. Cut both ends off flush with the whipping (fig. 3) and also remove any evidence of prior taping, tying or heat-sealing.

Method 2 – improved whipping
This eliminates the ugly bulge and chafing point that can be created by the elbows within a common whipping; it is also a little more secure. Using a small needle (as illustrated), or merely a separate loop of whipping twine, wrap tightly as shown (figs 1–2) and thread the working end through the needle or loop. Withdraw whichever one of these aids is being employed (fig. 3) and pull the working end tight. Cut both ends close to the completed whipping (fig. 4). The two ends will have half-knotted themselves beneath the wrapping turns (fig. 5).

Whipping method 1 – common whipping

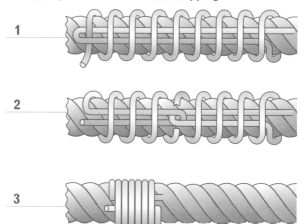

1

2

3

Whipping method 2 – improved whipping

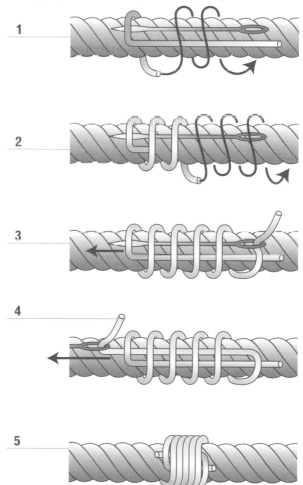

1

2

3

4

5

<33>

Method 3 – West Country whipping

Although not the neatest of whippings, this does at least stay on longer than those already described (which will unravel if a single turn is accidentally nicked and then breaks). Tie a half-knot (fig. 1) in the middle of the twine. Take both working ends around to the other side of the rope (fig. 2) and tie a second identical half-knot. Pull it tight (fig. 3). Go back to the beginning and tie a third half-knot alongside the first one (fig. 4). Then tie a fourth half-knot beside the second one (fig. 5). Repeat this process as often as necessary and finish with a reef (square) knot (fig. 6).

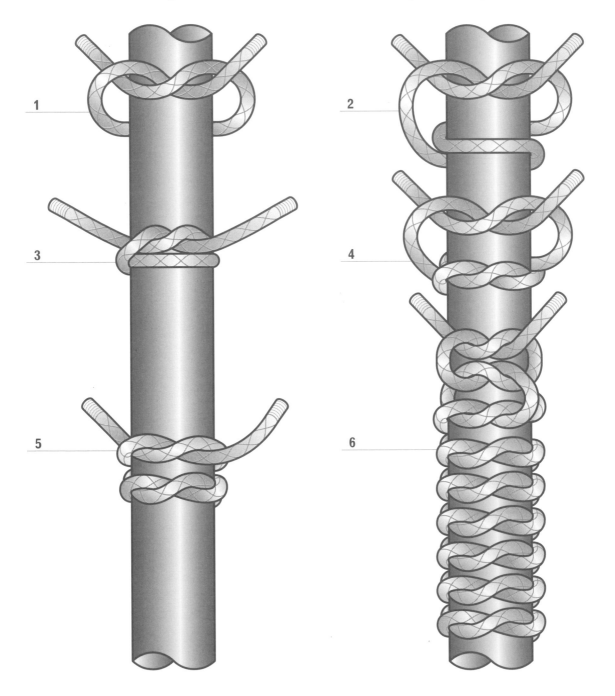

<34>

Method 4 – palm-and-needle whipping

A sewn whipping is a robust treatment for a rope's end. Use waxed twine, which may be doubled. Pass the needle and twine beneath a strand at the starting point, to anchor the standing end, and begin to bind (fig. 1). When the whipping is of a length equivalent to the rope's diameter, add riding turns that follow the three grooves between individual strands (figs 2–4).

Finally, take a securing turn around one of the riding turns, and pull it into the heart of the rope, before stitching the twine back and forth through the rope (fig. 5). Cut the end off flush against the rope (fig. 6). The riding turns not only hold this whipping tight to the rope's end, but also protect it from chafe. On braided rope they may – if preferred – be stitched parallel to one another along the length of the whipping (fig. 7).

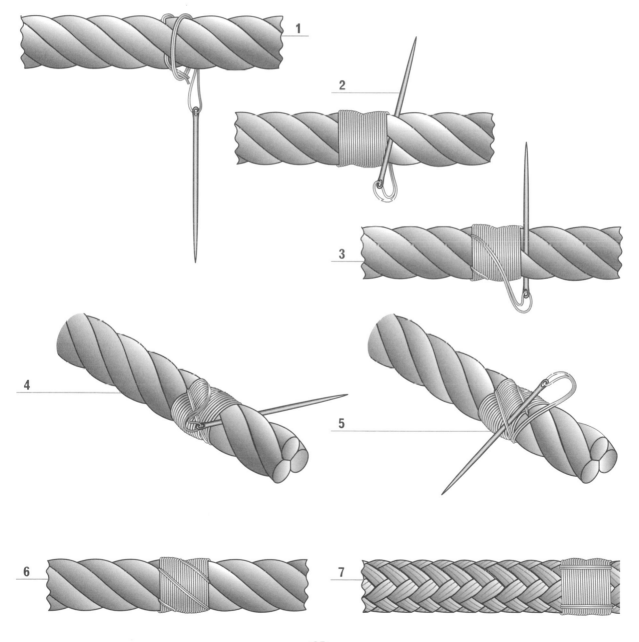

< 35 >

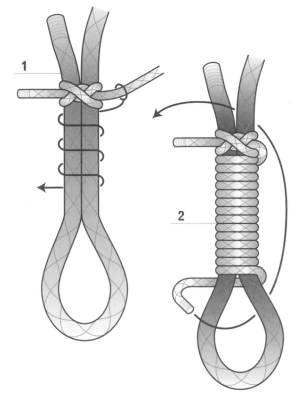

SEIZINGS

Wrapping turns, akin to whipping, and using the same twine, spunyarn or cord (depending on the size of the rope), can be used to make strong semi-permanent loops in rope or smaller cordage. They were used in the standing and running rigging of square-rigged ships, where they were obviously preferred to knots or splices.

Method 1 – simple seizing

Make a bight of the required size and tie the two parts together with a constrictor knot (fig. 1). Wrap a series of neat turns tightly towards the eye of the rope (fig. 2). Pass the working end through the eye, take it down the length of the seizing, and bring it up through the two rope parts at the other end (fig. 3). Tighten this turn and add a second in the same way (figs 4–5). Overriding turns that tension and secure in this way are known as frapping turns. Finally, insert the working end into, around and back out of the two taut frapping turns and pull down to create a knot that slides discreetly into the jaw of the seized eye (fig. 6).

Pull down
to tighten
knot

Method 2 – racking seizing

This is an even stronger treatment. Form an eye of the necessary size and apply a series of tight figure-of-eight turns (the 'racking'). No starting knot is required if the standing end of the twine is trapped within the V-shaped crossing points on one side of the racking turns (fig. 1). Return along the length of the half-completed seizing, wrapping the working end into the spaces between the previously laid racking turns (figs 2–3).

Apply two tight frapping turns (fig. 4). The knot already described for a simple seizing would be adequate; but, for a real belt-and-braces job, pull one frapping turn across the top of the other and – with a needle – tuck the working end as shown (fig. 5). Repeat this several times, until a three-part plait is created that goes up and down both sides of the seizing and between the two legs of the eye itself (fig. 6).

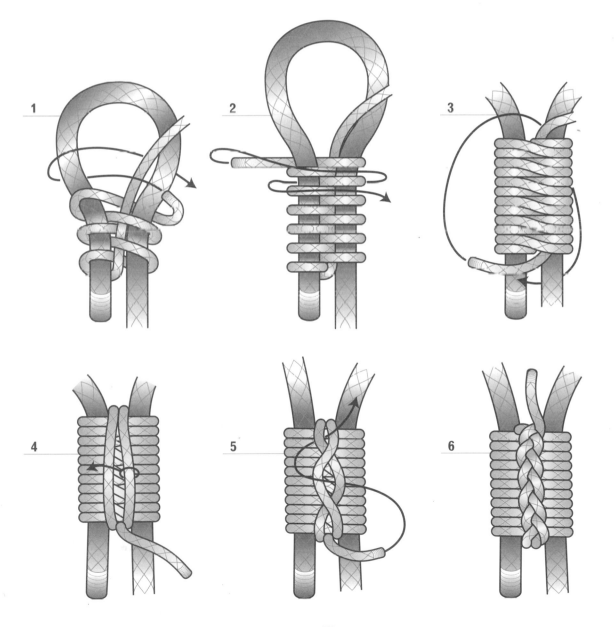

<37>

ON KNOTS

Part of the pleasure of going afloat lies in all the forward planning and preparation. This is when predictable snags should be foreseen and action taken to overcome them. Plan the sail, then sail the plan. The most versatile self-help kit to carry aboard is a lot of rope and all sorts of smaller cordage – but learn the knots to make them work. Practise them until they can be tied with your eyes shut, behind your back, and in every awkward attitude imaginable.

One vital commandment that experienced boating types exhort carefree younger ones to obey is: 'Use one hand for the job, keep the other for yourself.' In other words, when working on deck, always hold on. Furthermore, when working conditions turn impossible this axiom changes to: 'Both hands for yourself – and forgo the job for now.' Since many knot-tying tasks are two-handed ones, that is another reason for being prepared. When a weighted throwing line is required in

an emergency, it is too late to start tying a monkey's fist (see Other Useful Knots).

There are thousands of knots from which to acquire a useful repertoire, so which are considered most handy? In June 1999 the Surrey branch of the International Guild of Knot Tyers published a list of the six they had agreed ought to be taught first for use in modern ropes. Those knots are: figure-of-eight knot; sheet bend; bowline; constrictor; rolling hitch; and round turn and two half-hitches; and they further urged that the figure-of-eight knot (which can be modified to act as a stopper knot, loop, bend or hitch) should be taught first of all. The 'Surrey Six' is a sensible selection, although it does not have boating exclusively in mind, and all of them are included in this book. Other knotting practitioners might argue for a different clutch of knots. During my ten years as a London river policeman and frogman, I tied the killick hitch a lot (for salvage work and to recover drowned corpses), and the clove hitch (for tying up boats and as a means of hanging automobile tyre fenders); yet during those years I did not use the constrictor knot at all for work.

KNOT NAMES

Knotting nomenclature is haphazard. The name of a knot may say what it looks like; for example: a round turn and two half-hitches, a figure-of-eight knot, a square knot. It sometimes credits an individual group with its discovery or invention: Ashley's stopper knot, angler's loop. The name may indicate a knot's main use: reef knot, sheet bend, constrictor knot, bottle sling. Some names hint (rightly or wrongly) at a knot's history: the Alpine butterfly knot may have originated in Europe where it was used by mountaineers; the bowline and sheet bend have obvious sailing connections. But knot names can also be misleading: the fisherman's knot is often used as a bend, while the fisherman's bend is actually a hitch. And nobody knows for sure why the carrick bend is so named. Where an anecdote exists in connection with the name of any knot that appears in the following sections of this book, it will be recounted.

<38>

KNOT STRENGTH

If a knotted line breaks, it often does so close to the knot. This is due to a combination of factors. Sharp bends impose stresses and strains upon strands, while adjacent parts within a knot rub and may abrade (even cut) one another. Exactly what occurs is still not known for certain, and to learn all there is to know would take a working party of scientists and engineers from several fields (physics, chemistry, mechanics and mathematics). The fact that knots weaken rope has led to the practice of comparing a manufacturer's quoted breaking strengths for new ropes with the actual tested breaking strengths (invariably less) of specific knots in those lines. An overhand knot reduces that breaking strength by more than half of what it would otherwise be, and so its efficiency is said to be about 45 per cent; an unwanted overhand knot should be removed from any line as soon as it is discovered, before it becomes too tight to untie without lasting damage to the line, or causes it to part. The carrick bend – epitomized in seamanship manuals as a strong knot – is actually only about 65 per cent efficient; in other words, it reduces the breaking strength of

hawsers and cables by one-third. Hitches, with their gentler round turns, are generally much stronger, with efficiencies of around 80–85 per cent.

Very little research has been done on the breaking strengths of individual knots. Observation and guesswork, rough-and-ready experimentation, quite apart from the data generated from more controlled tests in the laboratories and factories of the ropemakers, have all so far proved inconclusive. Published facts and figures vary, and seem to depend upon the test rigs used by competing manufacturers, each of whom is (understandably) keen to out-do the opposition in the presentation of its products. It is therefore not always possible to compare like with like. For half a century, one knotting writer after another has listed the one-way sheet bend as 69 per cent efficient, but this very precise figure is almost certainly an average calculated from a battery of now outmoded test results. Without knowing precisely how the tests were conducted, no reliance can be placed upon that percentage. How the knot performs from day to day will depend upon the material in which it is tied – and what is then done to it.

<39>

Of course, a work-worn rope is already weakened, and this is a further factor in the sum to determine knot efficiency. A line that retains only 75 per cent of its original strength, into which a 65 per cent knot is then tied, will be reduced to 65 per cent of 75 per cent (about 50 per cent).

A steady pull on a rope is one thing – an abrupt snatch can render the manufacturer's calculated breaking strength meaningless. Momentum is a product of mass multiplied by direction and strength of pull. The short, steep swell from a passing tug in harbour can snap a yacht's mooring lines (breaking strength 10 tonnes) as easily as parcel twine; so can a wallowing tow that snatches at its towline. Rate of load is the critical factor in these instances; a knotted line that can barely handle a given strain for 60 seconds will need to be more than twice as strong to cope with an identical load applied over half that time – and will fail when it is almost instantaneous. That is why the authorities responsible for inspecting, testing and certifying fitness of purpose for safety harnesses, lifeboat falls and other vital working ropes and cordage may specify a safe working load as little as one-seventh of the known breaking strengths of the ropes in question.

Still, even the weakest synthetic lines have such a strength-to-weight ratio that – unless it is deliberately sacrificed for lightweight high performance – any question of cordage being badly impaired by knots is not such a consideration as it once was with natural-fibre ropes. Many synthetic lines on boats are, in fact, massively over-strength for what they are employed to do, for the simple reason that a thinner cord would be hard to grasp and haul, and because pulley blocks, sheaves and winches are not scaled down for the miniature diameters that might actually cope with the work involved. It is even reported that some tiny dinghies, designed to teach children to sail in not much more than a Force 3 breeze, have been needlessly rigged with immensely strong top-of-the-range Dyneema/Spectra cordage.

Fibre elasticity is probably the most important factor influencing knot strength, and – as nylon stretches most of all – it may be that nylon ropes make the strongest knots, with other ropes having knot strengths proportional to their elasticity. So knot strength is less of a clearcut concept than it is often supposed to be: it depends not only on what knot is tied, but also the material in which it is tied – and how it is executed. A carelessly worked knot will be weaker than a well-formed and tightened one.

KNOT SECURITY

Knots that slip, capsize or spill unintentionally, as a consequence of an inherently loose structure, are not weak but insecure. Strength and security are two separate considerations. A very secure knot (for example, the fisherman's knot) may be relatively weak because its nip is concentrated in a small area; the vice versa bend, with more turns and tucks over a larger area, is both strong and secure. Some knots, such as the common bowline tied in hard-laid stuff, are strong and secure enough when a steady load is applied, but spill if shaken by the wind or subjected to intermittent jerks. The bowline is made more secure in its alternative forms of double bowline and water bowline. The reason a granny knot is never recommended is because it is irredeemably weak and insecure. (The name of this knot never was, I trust, a slur on the knot-tying abilities of grandmothers, but rather is a derivation of 'granary knot', from its use in seizing the necks of grain sacks.)

Given that strength and security are different qualities, knots that combine both would seem to be ideal. Why use any other? Well, the simplest knot applicable to the job is best because it is the easiest to learn and remember, quickest to tie, and most readily untied again. This 'survival of the simplest' is a phenomenon that was pointed out by Pieter van de Griend[IGKT] in his booklet *Knots and Rope Problems* (1992). As he explained it, the filtering effects induced by learning (about rope problems) cause the simplest of solutions to survive. Then again, simple knots generally possess a distinctive and instantly

<40>

recognizable form. This is desirable so that crew members all know the same knots and are never confronted in a critical moment by an unfamiliar knotty conglomeration. But simplicity may be had only at the expense of friction, so choosing simple knots is a deliberate, calculated trade-off between strength and security. If a more elaborate knot is required, it should be used.

THE LAW OF LOOP, HITCH AND BIGHT

Some hitches can be untied by the simply expedient of sliding or lifting them off their point of attachment (like a clove hitch from a bollard). Bereft of its foundation, the knot falls apart and vanishes. Some loop knots, or knots made with loops – the sheepshank is an obvious one – also collapse if a single, crucial retaining bight is removed. All of the knots that can be untied in this fashion, without withdrawing an end, may also be tied in the bight – that is, without using an end.

Tying knots in the bight is very useful (and occasionally indispensable), since it makes possible rapid, almost sleight-of-hand tying methods; and where both ends of a line are otherwise anchored or occupied, it is the only way to tie some knots. Put briefly, if a knot can be untied in the bight, it can be tied in the bight. This unsuspected natural law of loop, hitch and bight was identified by a retired research scientist, the late Dr Harry Asher [IGKT], who published it first in *A New System of Knotting – Volume II* (1986) and then later in *The Alternative Knot Book* (1989). Self-evident, once it has been pointed out, the law enables knot tyers to look for quicker and slicker methods of tying knots – and to know when not to bother. For instance, the knotted form of both constrictor and strangle knots is almost identical: only the direction of their diagonals is different. Yet the constrictor knot can be tied in the bight, while the strangle knot cannot.

TYING KNOTS

A knot is either right or wrong. One mistaken tuck or turn results in a different knot entirely, or no knot at all. A take-it-or-leave-it attitude to knotting afloat is unacceptable, since wind and tides will seek out mistakes and punish them.

A knot is as good as the cordage in which it is tied. Shock elastics (bungee cords) shed normally reliable old favourites like the bowline, but retain others such as the angler's loop. All but the simplest knots must be systematically worked snug, a bit at a time, prior to final tightening. Very few knots (the reef knot is one) can be tightened by merely pulling both ends. Others must be kneaded into shape, with slack worked through and out of them a bit at a time – gradually eliminating any daylight that peeks between the various knot parts – until it is possible to apply a final tightening pull. Even then, it is generally necessary to do so evenly to each working end and standing part in turn, however many there are (the triple figure-of-eight loop has eight). In describing the method of tying each knot in this book, it is not unwanted wordiness if instructions say 'work snug and then tighten'.

<41>

STOPPERS, BINDINGS AND SHORTENINGS

There's nothing like watching your jib sheet disappear through the block whilst hurtling along ... to make you wish you had brushed up on your stopper knots.

Nola Trower[IGKT], *Knots and Ropework* (1992)

Quite apart from its general use to denote any entanglement – deliberate or accidental – in a length of line, the word 'knot' means something specific to proficient knot tyers. Anything other than a bend or hitch is a knot, and this includes stopper knots, binding knots and shortenings. Stopper knots should be tied in the ends of jib sheets and main sheets, together with any other line that must be prevented from pulling out of a tackle, block or fairlead. Binding knots are essentially for bundles – sails, kitbags, bandages or an unwieldy load of oars and spars. Shortenings either take up unwanted slack or are modified to act as tensioning devices (see also Other Useful Knots).

Knots, bends and hitches tied in string, twine, fishing line or other thin stuff are also referred to as mere 'knots'; and, in this respect, the criterion seems to be whether or not it can be easily untied and the line re-used – if not, it is a knot.

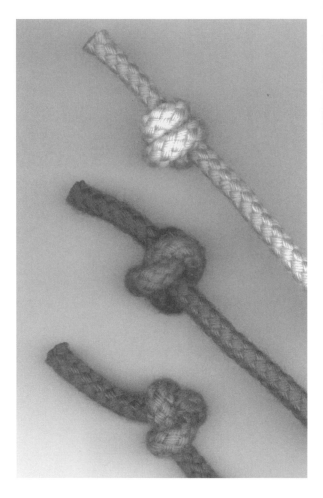

DOUBLE OVERHAND KNOT

APPLICATIONS

This compact stopper knot may be used in the smallest-diameter threads or larger cords with the advantage that the end is aligned neatly with the standing part. It is also a technique fundamental to tying some other knots (for example, the strangle knot) and bends (the double fisherman's knot), and should be learnt for that reason.

METHOD

Tie an overhand knot (fig. 1) and tuck the working end a second time (fig. 2). Pull gently on both ends, and as the knot tightens it will begin to wrap around itself (fig. 3). Actively twiddle both knot parts, held in the fingers, in opposite directions as indicated, to make this happen. Then pull the knot tight (fig. 4).

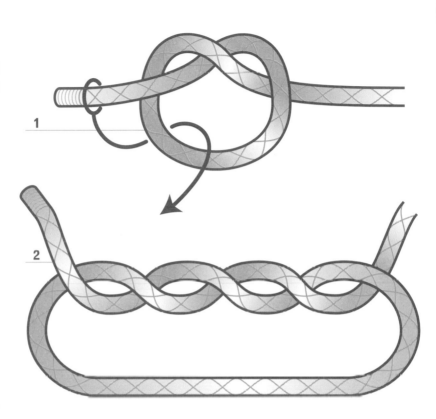

1

2

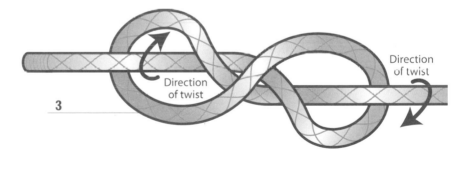

3

Direction of twist

Direction of twist

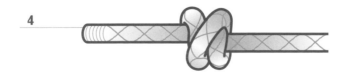

4

<45>

FIGURE-OF-EIGHT KNOT

APPLICATIONS

This is the popular stopper knot seen in the ends of most jib sheets and main sheets. Use it also on halyards, boom vangs, kicking straps, and the end of any other rope that passes through a block or fitting from which it must not escape, including dinghy davits. It will not block a larger aperture than an overhand knot (since both knots encircle their standing parts with the same hare-lip imperfection), but it can be easily untied after use – when the overhand knot is likely to be irretrievably jammed.

METHOD

Form a loop (fig. 1) and impart an extra twist. Tuck the end (fig. 2) and draw the knot up fairly snug (fig. 3) to create the flattish figure-of-eight layout. Finally, push up against the knot to create the surrounding collar characteristic of stopper knots (fig. 4). For knots that will not have to endure rough treatment, consider incorporating a draw-loop (figs 5–6).

HISTORY

The name 'figure-of-eight knot' first appears in the *Young Officer's Sheet Anchor* (1808) by Darcy Lever. The alternative name for it in that period was the Flemish knot. This versatile knot can be modified to serve as a loop, bend or hitch, and for this reason not only is it one of the select batch of six knots recommended for use in modern ropes by the IGKT Surrey branch, but they urge that it should be the first knot taught.

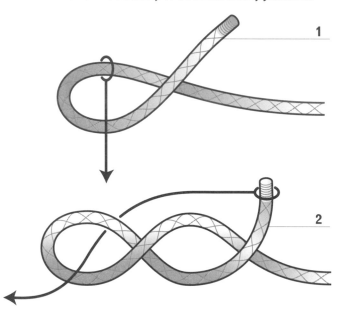

1

2

3

5

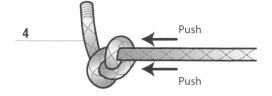

4

Push

Push

6

<46>

ASHLEY'S STOPPER KNOT

APPLICATIONS

When a figure-of-eight knot is too small to block a hole or slot, this is the bulkier alternative.

METHOD

Tie a simple noose or slip-knot (figs 1–2) and pull it tight. Tuck the working end exactly as shown (fig. 3) and then pull on the standing part of the line to reduce the loop until it traps and holds the end (fig. 4). On the underside of the knot, a distinctive three-part crown of knot parts surrounds the standing part of the line (fig. 5).

HISTORY

Some time before 1910, American artist Clifford Warren Ashley was aboard the *Mattie Flavel* in Delaware Bay, drawing illustrations of oyster culture for *Harper's Magazine*, when he spotted a huge knot (too large, he thought, to be a figure-of-eight knot) on the foresail halyard of a Chesapeake ketch that overtook him. Nobody he asked could identify it, so he set about replicating it – and this was the result, which he named the oysterman's stopper knot. A few days later, in the settlement of Bivalve, the same boat tied up nearby; on going aboard, Ashley found that the stopper knot in question was nothing more than a wet and swollen figure-of-eight knot tied in a work-worn old rope. This was his first bit of inventive knot tying, but he would go on to become the renowned author of *The Ashley Book of Knots* (1944), a monumental work that is every avid knot tyer's bible, while Ashley's stopper knot has established itself as a minor classic in the knotting repertoire.

1

2

Pull to tighten

Pull to tighten

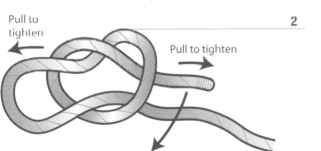

3

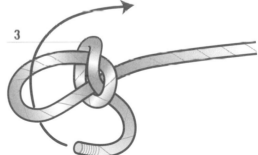

4

Push   Pull to tighten

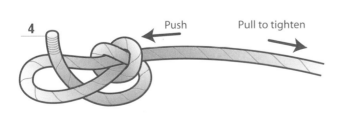

5

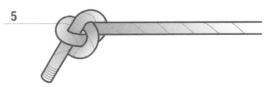

<47>

CONSTRICTOR KNOT

APPLICATIONS

Use one or more of these knots as a temporary whipping on a rope's end, to begin a seizing, as a substitute for hose clamps, to repair a cracked tiller, or to tie a pencil to a clipboard. As a bag or sack knot, tie it with a quick-release draw-loop. It also serves to hold objects being glued together. On soft foundations such as rope, use hard-laid line. For unyielding ones, such as metal rails or rings, use soft and stretchy stuff. Either way the knot will cling and grip like a boa constrictor. There are several different ways in which to tie a constrictor knot.

METHOD 1 – TIED WITH AN END

Tie a clove hitch and then knot the two standing parts with a half-knot (figs 1–3). Pull the resulting knot as tight as possible, so that the overlying diagonal strongly reinforces the entwined knot parts (fig. 4). For semi-permanent bindings, attach each end of the cord to a fid (or a pair of winch handles, screwdrivers, spanners or other robust objects), and pull them strenuously apart with both hands and feet; or, if possible, use two opposing cockpit winches. Cut the ends off close to the knot.

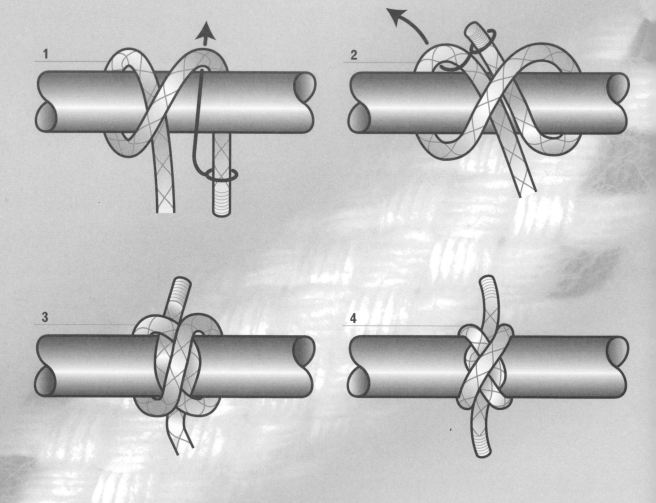

<48>

HISTORY

A knot that may have been the constrictor knot was described, but regrettably not illustrated, in the 1st century AD by the ancient Greek physician Heraklas for use as a surgical sling. There is similar circumstantial evidence that it was the so-called gunner's knot with which the necks of flannel bags containing gunpowder were seized to make cartridges for muzzle-loading field guns. In 1916 it appeared in the Swedish book *Om Knutar* by Hjalmar Öhrvall as the timber knot. It was also published and illustrated in *Solmukirja* (1931) by the Finnish girl scout leader Martta Ropponen, who had been introduced to it by a Spaniard, Raphael Gaston, who knew it as a whip knot used by muleteers and herdsmen in the mountains of Spain. They corresponded – so the story goes – in Esperanto. The knot was popularized by Clifford W. Ashley in 1944. It is another of the 'Surrey Six' knots mentioned before.

METHOD 2 – TIED IN THE BIGHT

It is quicker and easier to tie this knot in the bight, provided the end of whatever is to be bound is accessible. Take a turn (fig. 1), pull out a bight (fig. 2) and, imparting half a twist, pass it over the end of the foundation (fig. 3). Pull tight, as before, and cut the ends off short.

1

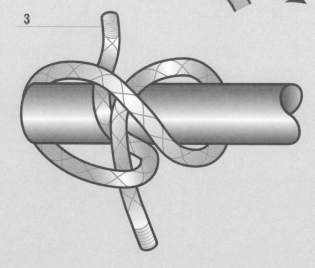

2

3

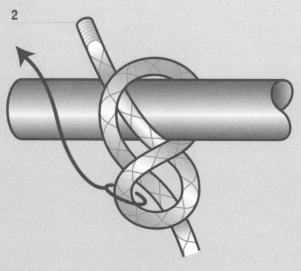

<49>

METHOD 3

Lay the twine or cord down on the deck, a thwart or other convenient working surface, so that it takes the shape of a written ampersand (&) (fig. 1), and insert the object to be seized as shown (fig. 2).

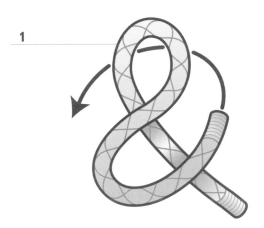

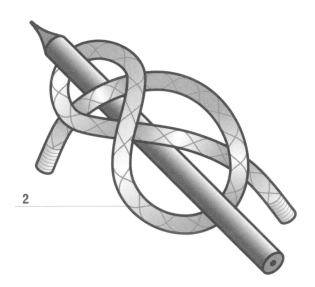

METHOD 4

Lay the twine or cord down in the form of a flattened 'Z' (fig. 1) and rearrange it as shown (fig. 2). Pick up as described for method 3 above.

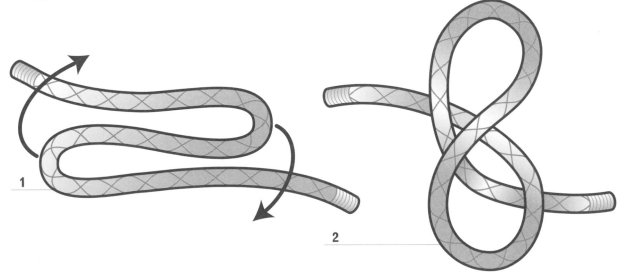

<50>

CONSTRICTOR KNOT WITH DRAW-LOOP

APPLICATIONS

Usually a constrictor knot must be cut off when it is no longer required. To do so, simply sever the overlying diagonal using a sharp blade, when the knot will fall away in two curly segments without damage to whatever was held within the binding. If only a temporary seizing is needed, however, add a draw-loop.

METHOD

Take a crossing turn and insert a bight over one knot part and under two more (fig. 1). Pull tight (fig. 2).

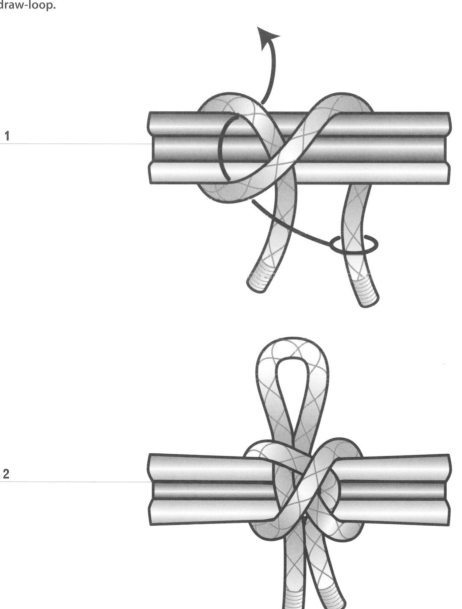

1

2

DOUBLE CONSTRICTOR KNOT

APPLICATIONS

As the diameter of an object increases, the efficacy of a constrictor knot is slightly impaired, but this knot rectifies the deficiency.

METHOD 1 – TIED WITH AN END

Begin the knot in the usual way, adding a second turn prior to the final tuck (fig. 1). Pull tight (fig. 2).

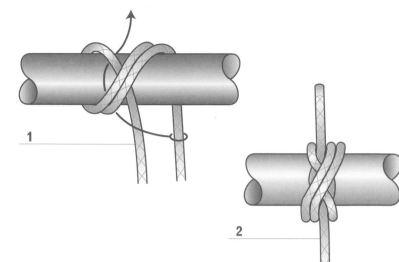

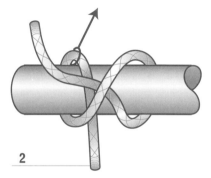

METHOD 2 – TIED IN THE BIGHT

First make a clove hitch (fig. 1). Swap the upper one of the two ends for the left-hand loop (fig. 2), withdraw a bight (fig. 3) and, with half a twist, pass it over the end of the object to be seized and pull all tight (fig. 4).

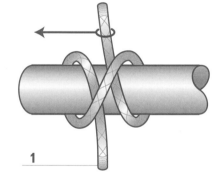

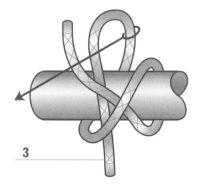

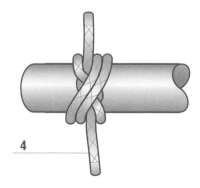

<52>

STRANGLE KNOT

APPLICATIONS

This knot makes a compact or streamlined alternative to the constrictor knot. It is more easily tightened by hand than the constrictor (but jams a trifle less fiercely).

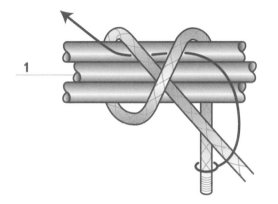

1

METHOD 1 – DIRECT

Wrap a crossing turn around the foundation and tuck as shown (fig. 1). Pull the knot tight (fig. 2).

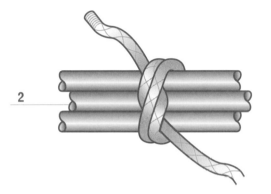

2

METHOD 2 – INDIRECT

Tie a double overhand knot (figs 1–2), then fold it into a bracelet and slide it over the object to be contained (fig. 3).

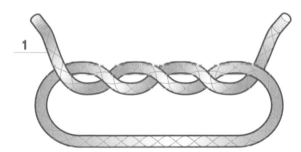

1

2

HISTORY

In his book *Om Knutar* (1916), Swedish writer Hjalmar Öhrvall preferred this knot to the constrictor because its turns lie more snugly together; and an IGKT member writing in the Guild's quarterly magazine *Knotting Matters* under the nautical pen-name of Jack Fidspike enthused in 1997. 'The aptly named Constrictor will cling and grip like glue, Sir! While the Strangle Knot's a stricture some deem neater and no looser.'

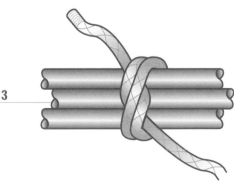

3

<53>

JUG, JAR OR BOTTLE SLING

APPLICATIONS

Containers of liquids are always heavy for their size. To hang, carry or drag around anything from a water demijohn to a bottle of one's favourite beverage, a carboy of battery acid – or even a salvaged Greek or Roman amphora – use this ratchet-like interwoven collar with its twin handles of cord.

METHOD

Make two overlapping loops and pull the knot part indicated under/over/under/over as shown (fig. 1). Locate the bight beneath the knot layout (fig. 2) and pull it down. Then similarly locate the bight on top of the knot (fig. 3) and pull that down. Manipulate the completed knot to even out the tension and ensure symmetry (fig. 4). Place the resulting circular plaited bracelet over and around the neck of the jug, jar or bottle and pull it tight. Keep the bight small, and one of the two loose lengths of line much longer than the other. Insert one of them through the bight before knotting both with either a tape (water) knot or a fisherman's knot (fig. 5). This way, the two handles will instantly adjust to the same size when picked up. For a cleverer system, try Asher's equalizer (figs 6–7).

1

2

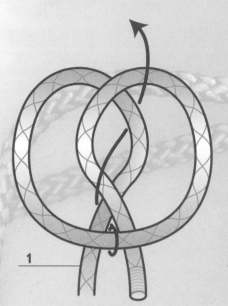

3

4

<54>

HISTORY

In his *Log Book Notes*
(1889), E.N. Little refers to this
knot as a jar sling knot; Johann
Röding, author of *Allgemeines Wörterbuch
der Marine* (1795) called it a jug sling. But
the earliest description seems to have been
in the 1st century AD, by that obscure
ancient Greek physician named Heraklas,
for use as a surgical sling. Asher's
equalizer was invented in the
mid-1980s by Dr Harry
Asher[IGKT].

<55>

REEF KNOT (SQUARE KNOT)

APPLICATIONS

This is a binding knot for tying up parcels of all kinds, from first aid bandages to shortened sails in craft that still have cord reef points. Use it also to fasten gaskets around furled sails or to tie off laced sail covers, as well as to fasten down an anchor on deck. Its security depends in part upon it pressing against whatever it encloses. Never use it as a bend, for which purpose it would be unreliable and therefore dangerous.

METHOD

Place one working end on top of the other and tie a half-knot; then place the same end on top of the other again and add a second half-knot (figs 1–2). Remember: 'Left over right, then right over left.' Observe the layout of the completed knot, which consists of two half-knots (with opposing helixes, one left-handed and the other right-handed). Alternatively, it may be regarded as two interlocked bights. The working ends must emerge on the same side of the knot. Pull it tight (fig. 3). In shoe laces it is usual to leave a pair of draw-loops, making a double reef bow (not illustrated); but for tasks afloat, a slipped reef knot (fig. 4), with a single draw-loop in one end only, is easier to tie and comes adrift less often.

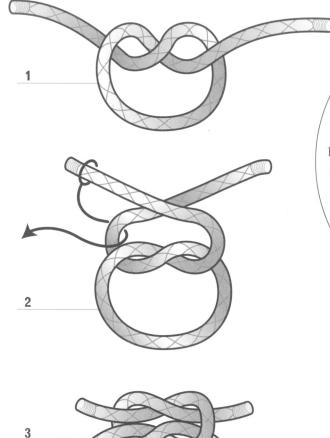

1

2

3

HISTORY

The ancient Greeks, Romans and Egyptians all knew this knot and were aware that it was superior to the unreliable granny knot (which both slips and jams). The Romans knew it as the Hercules knot, and the Roman scientist and historian Pliny the Elder (AD 23–79) made an odd claim for it: he wrote in his Natural History that wounds bound with this knot healed quicker. Today, first aid instructors still teach that it is the knot for bandages and slings, although I doubt if one in a hundred knows the underlying reason why.

4

<56>

POLE HITCH

APPLICATIONS

A couple of these bindings will tame an awkward armful of oars and hitchers (boathooks), spinnaker poles, masts and spars, or other incompatible bits and pieces.

METHOD

Lay out twin bights of cordage beneath the objects to be tied together (fig. 1) and tuck an end through each one (fig. 2). Pull the arrangement tight in such a way that both bights and ends are close together (fig. 3) and secure with a reef knot (fig. 4). Repeat at the other end of the load.

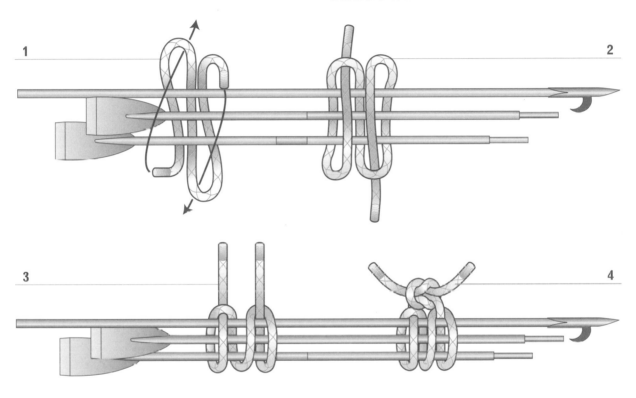

HISTORY

The name pole hitch appeared in 1987 in *Knotting for Guides* by Hazel Bailey. Clifford W. Ashley identified it as a means for a carpenter to sling a plank or joist on edge (presumably on a construction site) or flat as a painting platform (when it is known as a scaffold hitch). It is actually a slack, deformed clove hitch (see Hitches) and may be tied that way.

<57>

SHEEPSHANK

APPLICATIONS

Use this knot to shorten a rope without adjusting its ends. It will also bridge a damaged section of line, enabling it to be used (with care and caution) until a replacement can be obtained, or may be employed simply to hang up an intrusive length of line that is too short to be coiled.

METHOD 1 – DIRECT

Lay the rope into a long 'S' (or 'Z') shape (fig. 1) and apply a half-hitch over the end of each bight (fig. 2). This is a most insecure knot and, unless the working line is held under tension, it can fall apart; or, if tied in soft-laid flexible line, the bight may turn over until it spills its half-hitch. To overcome these failings, pass each standing part of the line through the nearest bight, or – if tying in the bight is advantageous – simply add a second half-hitch at each end (fig. 3). Another secure version uses a couple of strangle knots (fig. 4).

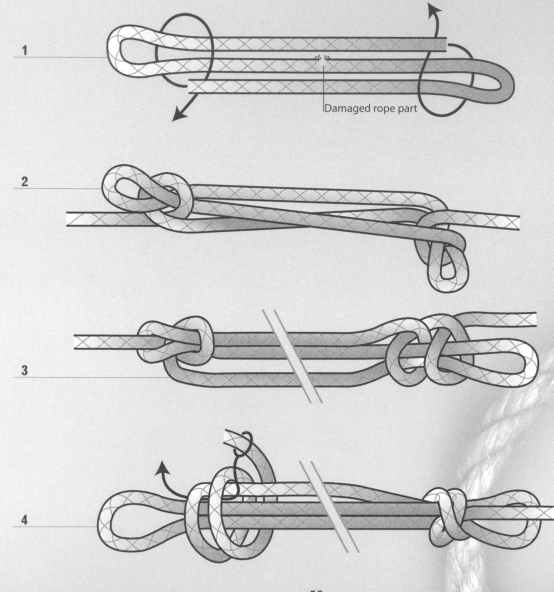

1

Damaged rope part

2

3

4

<58>

METHOD 2 – INDIRECT

Instead of passing each end bight through a pre-formed half-hitch (fig. 1), which is the usual way to tie a sheepshank, a half-hitch may be tied with the bight (fig. 2) and then pulled and rolled into the single standing part (figs 3–4). In this way a slack line that is already anchored at both ends may be tensioned.

1

2

3

4

HISTORY

One hoary tale has it that a sheepshank once tethered sheep to stakes so as to restrict them to individual grazing areas; then, as each circular patch was cropped bare, an animal's line could be lengthened to bring more grass within its reach. But the knot may have been so called merely because of a fancied likeness to a sheep's leg (or leg bone). Many accomplished knot tyers claim never to have used one in a long lifetime of working with rope; and Felix Reisenberg, writing in the first quarter of the 20th century, expressed his own doubts about the sheepshank when he observed drily that it was used about as much as a crossbow. But to disregard or view with disapproval any knot is shortsighted. For, as Clifford W. Ashley wrote in *The Ashley Book of Knots* (1944): 'Old knots long out of use have a way of coming back into this workaday world with renewed vigour and usefulness.'

<59>

single, double and triple loops

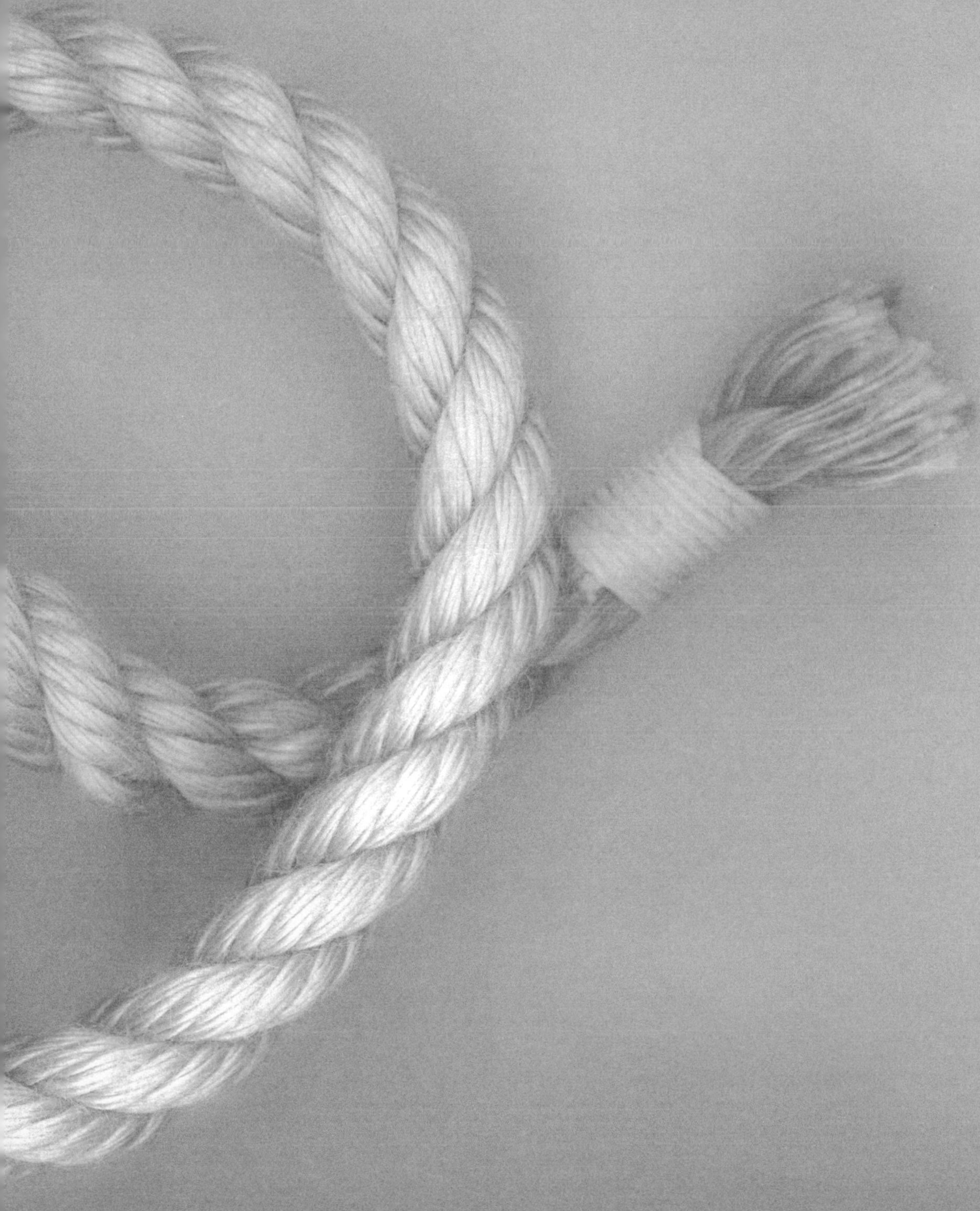

SINGLE, DOUBLE AND TRIPLE LOOPS

A loop knot ... serves much the same purpose as a hitch ... But ... it is possible to use a loop knot over and over again, which is the particular merit of the knot.

Clifford W. Ashley, *The Ashley Book of Knots* (1944)

The other main knot category is loops – single, double or triple (some of which are fixed, others sliding). Single-loop knots are used, more often than not, as handy alternatives to hitches ('A bowline on a bollard is the best of journey's ends,' wrote A.P. Herbert in his poem 'The Bowline is the King of Knots'). They can also

be interlocked to join two lines (see Bends). In these health-and-safety conscious times, with hazardous working practices strictly regulated by legislation, I do not recommend any ad hoc rope slings and chairs for regular working aloft, up for'ard or over the side. There are approved harnesses, tested and certificated, for the sensible and prudent, which it would be misguided to ignore. But all sailors sooner or later are confronted with the need for some urgent improvisation, when one or other of the multi-loop knots in this section may be employed as a makeshift chair knot for emergency repairs and rescue situations.

<62>

MIDSHIPMAN'S HITCH

APPLICATIONS

Use this slide-and-grip knot to make an adjustable single loop for the ends of moorings, guy-lines and so on, where an alteration in length or tension may be required periodically to cope with rising and falling tides, humidity and rainfall.

METHOD

Make a loop (fig. 1) and take a crossing turn around the standing part of the line (fig. 2). Add a second crossing turn, making sure to squeeze it between the initial diagonal and the upper part of the loop, before finishing off with a half-hitch around the standing part (fig. 3). When the knot has been tightened, it can be slid along the line by hand, but once the load is applied it holds firm. This is due to a dog's-leg deformation that the knot creates in the standing part of the line (fig. 4). It may also act as a shock-absorber, slipping to dissipate the energy of an unacceptable sudden load, until the load becomes manageable (when it will grip again).

HISTORY

The name implies an origin aboard His or Her Majesty's ships of war; and, as the rank of midshipman was a lowly one, it may be that it was a derogatory term for an underrated knot. In fact, it is a versatile and reliable slide and grip loop.

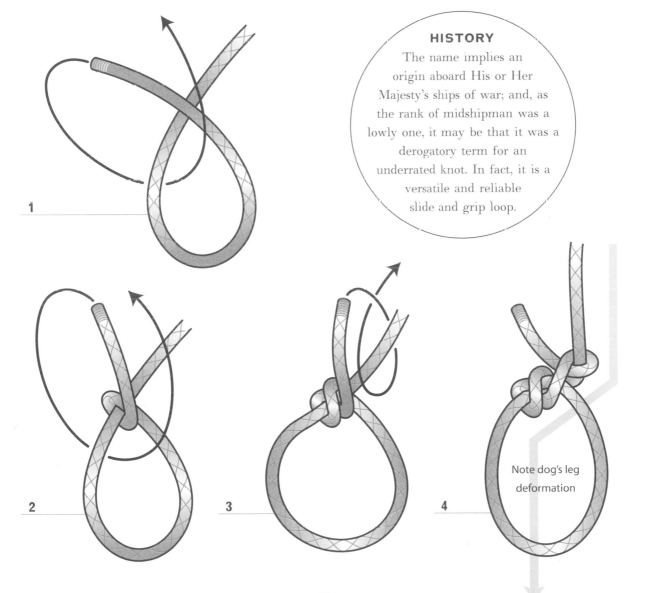

1

2

3

4

Note dog's leg deformation

<63>

BOWLINE

APPLICATIONS

The bowline (pronounced 'boh-linn') is universally used afloat for anything and everything that can be adequately done with a fixed single loop. It will also attach jib sheets and halyards to sails. And, subject to the caution already given about using tested safety harnesses whenever possible, it will go around a person's waist as a reassuring support and tether while they work over the side. Two interlocked bowlines also make a useful hawser bend (see Bends).

METHOD 1 – DIRECT

To tie the knot directly by what is called the sailor's method, make a loop (fig. 1) and, with a smooth turn of the wrist and hand (palm down to palm up), pass the working end down, around and up through, at the same time rolling the original loop into the standing part of the line (fig. 2). Take the working end behind the standing part and tuck it as shown (figs 3–4). Tighten the knot, leaving a longish end which in most instances ought to be at least the length of the final loop (fig. 5).

<64>

METHOD 2 – INDIRECT

Faced with someone overboard, or a mooring buoy gently but inexorably moving away from the boat, it can be necessary to tie a bowline this way – leaning outboard at full stretch (perhaps overbalancing, with someone else hanging on to one's legs). Pass the working end around or through the attachment point and tie a half-hitch with it (fig. 1). Then roll or trip this half-hitch into the standing part (figs 2–3) by straightening out the working end, and tuck as usual to complete the knot (fig. 4).

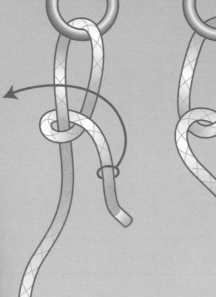

HISTORY

The knot is mentioned as a seafarer's knot by Sir Henry Mainwaring in *The Seaman's Dictionary* (1644) and illustrated in *Elements and Practice of Rigging and Seamanship* (1794) by David Steel. They knew it literally as a 'bow line knot' (from which its present name evolved), used to hold the weather leech of a square sail forward, closer to the wind, so as to prevent it being taken aback (inadvertently blown inside out), by tying it with a line brought from the bow of the ship. It is one of the 'Surrey Six' knots already mentioned. In the 1960s, this was the knot that we Metropolitan Police frogmen used to attach a dual-purpose lifeline and signal line around our waists, with a long end that was then dogged (tucked and wound several times around the adjacent loop leg) for extra security. It is a classic tried-and-trusted knot; William P. Maclean, in his book *Modern Marlinspike Seamanship* (1979), wrote: '... I would be happier if everyone could tie some kind of bowline. The number of sailors who cannot make a bowline at all is disgraceful.'

<65>

DOUBLE BOWLINE
(ROUND TURN BOWLINE)

APPLICATIONS

Despite its ready acceptance aboard most craft, the common bowline is far from being the strongest or most secure of loop knots. It is perhaps only 65 per cent efficient and can shake loose from hard-laid ropes. To improve it in both respects, particularly in stiff or slippery stuff, use this variant.

METHOD

First make a double turn (fig. 1), then tuck and tighten as for a common bowline (fig. 2).

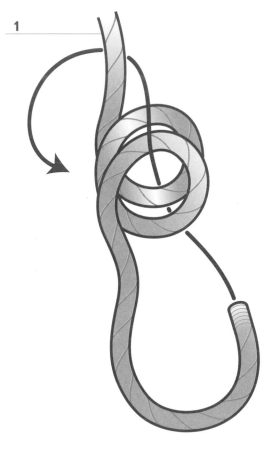

<66>

WATER BOWLINE

APPLICATIONS

This alternative to the double (or round turn) bowline is recommended for towing through water or dragging over rough terrain.

METHOD

Make two identical loops (fig. 1), then tuck and tighten as for the common bowline (fig. 2).

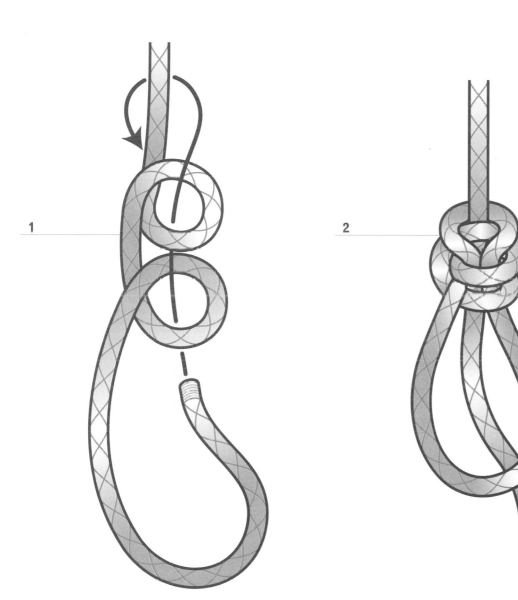

1

2

<67>

BOWLINE IN THE BIGHT

APPLICATIONS

This is one of those knots which – subject to the caution given at the beginning of this section – might be used to lower or hoist up a person, who (if conscious and capable) must thrust one leg through each loop and hold tightly on to the standing part of the rope at chest level.

METHOD

Make a long bight and begin with the doubled rope as if tying an orthodox bowline (fig. 1). But then bend the single working bight down, lift the two larger standing loops up through it (fig. 2), and allow the single bight to go back up again. The completed knot will be doubled throughout, except for the single bight around the standing parts (fig. 3).

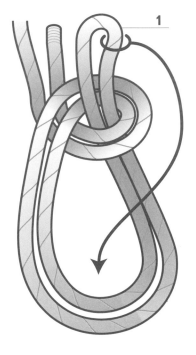

1

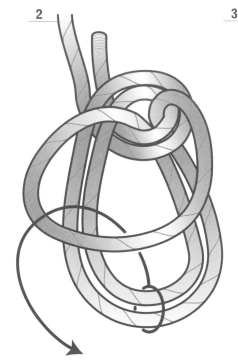

2

3

HISTORY

This knot was illustrated in *Allgemeines Wörterbuch der Marine* (1795) by Johann Röding, and it was referred to as the bowline upon the bight in the *Young Officer's Sheet Anchor* (1808) by Darcy Lever.

<68>

TRIPLE BOWLINE

APPLICATIONS

Bearing in mind the caution at the beginning of this section, a triple bowline may be employed as a seat sling or harness, with a loop carefully adjusted to fit each leg and an extra one to go around the person's chest and armpits.

METHOD

Using a long bight, tie the doubled line as if making an orthodox bowline (figs 1–2).

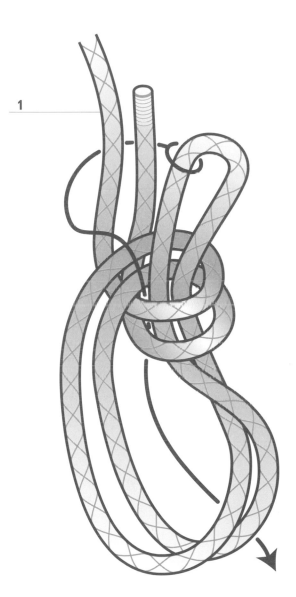

ANGLER'S LOOP

APPLICATIONS
This useful knot makes a relatively strong and very secure fixed loop in anything from the finest synthetic monofilaments to huge hawsers and cables. It even holds in shock elastics (bungee cord).

METHOD 1 – TIED IN AN END
Make an overhand knot with draw-loop and then tuck the working end as shown (figs 1–2). Work the knot snug and tight. It has a characteristic and easily recognizable finished form (figs 3–4).

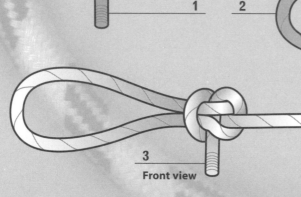

3
Front view

4
Rear view

METHOD 2 – TIED IN THE BIGHT
Once the finished form is familiar, adopt this faster method (figs 1–3).

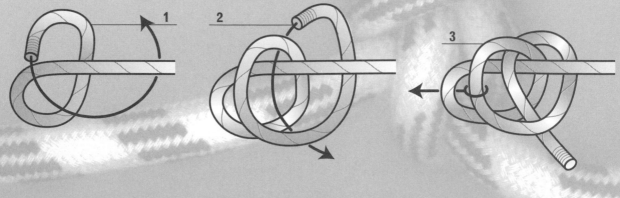

<70>

HISTORY

Whether or not this knot dates back
to the 17th century and the angling author
Izaak Walton, as some claim, is uncertain. In *Anglers'*
Knots in Gut and Nylon (1948), Stanley Barnes labelled it
a 'blood loop', a most misleading name as it is unrelated to the
blood knot family. It has also been described in print as the
'perfection loop'. Seamen seem not to have liked it because of its
tendency to jam in wet natural-fibre ropes, but it is ideal for use with
synthetic ropes and cordage. In 1985 while one of a group
circumnavigating the Isle of Wight, off the south coast of England, in sea
kayaks, I used these knots to fasten the deck elastics (of bungee cord) that
held bags containing my charts, waterproofs, sun hat and glasses, glucose
tablets and drinks, within easy reach outside my spray cover. Swamped
and tugged by the occasional wave, then dried out by the sun and
wind, the cords did not shift a millimetre during the trip (although
an instructor had earlier advised me to use self-amalgamating
tape, because – he said – deck elastics were impossible to
knot); our professional leader was amused to see how I
had tied port and starboard versions of the
knots, so that all the short ends were
streamlined to point aft.

1

METHOD 3

Revert to an adaptation of method 1 in order to attach
a line by this knot to a fixed anchorage point (figs 1–2).

2

<71>

ALPINE BUTTERFLY KNOT

APPLICATIONS

Tied handily in the bight, this is a fixed-loop knot used primarily to provide a clip-on point in safety lines, and may be pulled in any direction without undue distortion. It also enables temporary use of a damaged rope (when it becomes, effectively, a bend) by bridging the weakened section.

METHOD

There are several ways to tie this knot, but the one shown (with its leap-frog sequence) is possibly the most easily learnt. Take two round turns and transfer the right-hand part to the middle (fig. 1). Transfer the new right-hand part across to the extreme left-hand side (fig. 2) and then pull a bight through beneath the two remaining knot parts (figs 3–4). The resulting loop knot is symmetrical (fig. 5). Work it snug and tight (fig. 6).

1

2

HISTORY

This is a reputable old mountaineering knot, and — from its name — presumably of European origin. 'If the bowline is the King of knots,' wrote John Sweet in *Scout Pioneering* (1974), 'this must surely be the Queen.'

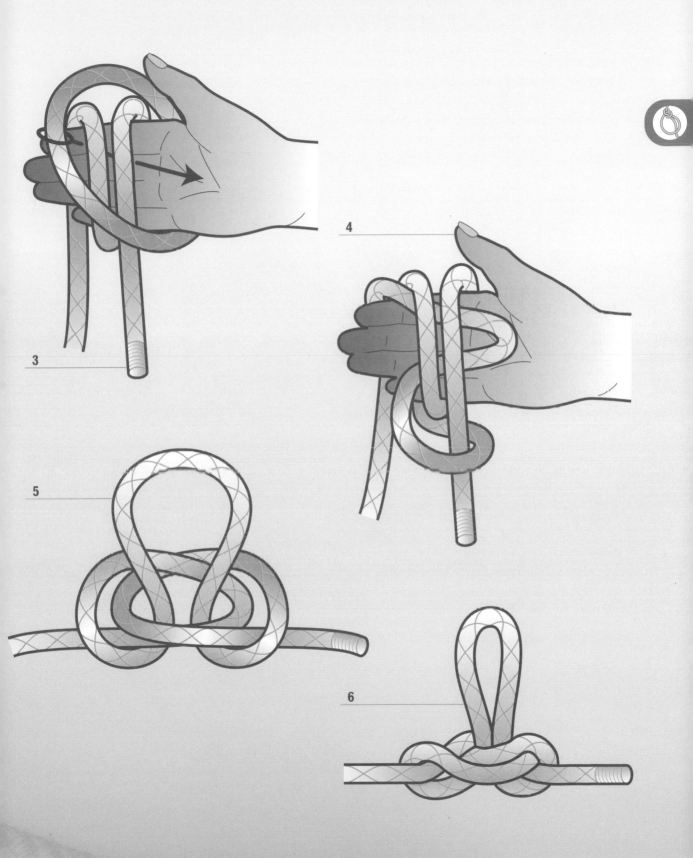

<73>

FIGURE-OF-EIGHT LOOP

APPLICATIONS

The figure-of-eight loop is one of those climbers' knots that ran away to sea. It is preferred by some to the classic bowline because it is easier to teach, tie and later remember correctly when cold, wet and exhausted (mentally as well as physically).

METHOD

With a long bight, tie a figure-of-eight knot in the doubled cord or rope (figs 1–2). As the knot is worked snug, prior to final tightening, rearrange the flat and parallel (train or tram lines) layout (fig. 3) so that the knot parts cross at each major curve to produce a more compact knot (figs 4–5). Contrive it so that the standing part of the line, upon which the load will be imposed, forms the outer bight at the loop end of the knot, since it may be stronger that way.

HISTORY

Also known as the Flemish loop, this knot was viewed with disfavour by sailors using natural-fibre ropes, in which it tended to jam when wet. It is, of course, based upon the figure-of-eight stopper knot (which is one of the 'Surrey Six' knots).

1

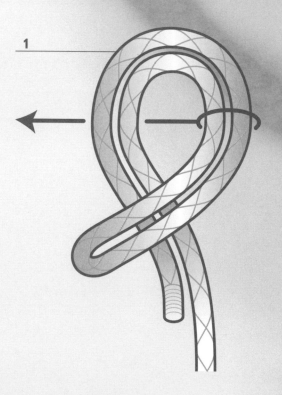

2

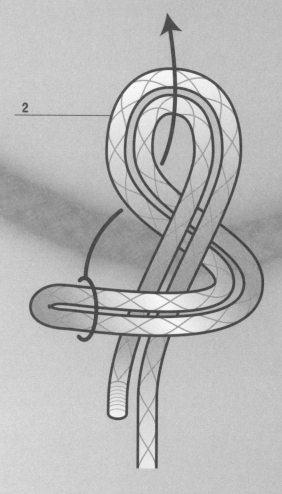

<74>

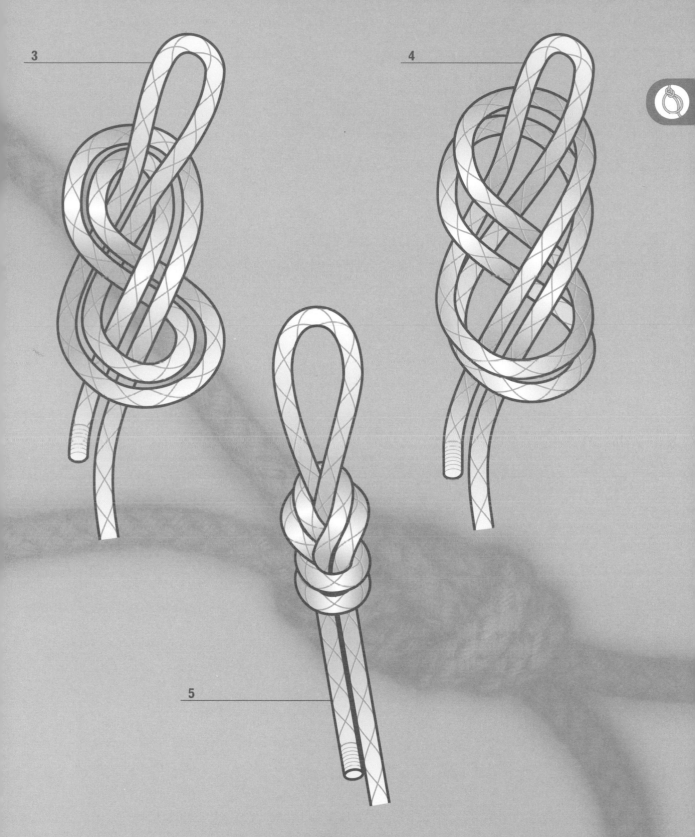

3

4

5

<75>

DOUBLE FIGURE-OF-EIGHT LOOP

APPLICATIONS

Chunkier than a bowline in the bight, this knot is a trifle stronger. Use it in the same way.

METHOD

With a long bight, use the doubled line to tie a figure-of-eight knot with a draw-loop (figs 1–2). Bring the upper bight down and lift the two lower bights up through it (fig. 3). Work the knot snug, with loop sizes as required, and then tighten it (fig. 4).

1

2

3

HISTORY

The double figure-of-eight loop seems to have been described first by Clifford W. Ashley in *The Ashley Book of Knots* (1944).

4

<76>

TRIPLE FIGURE-OF-EIGHT LOOP

APPLICATIONS
Use this like a triple bowline.

METHOD
Begin as for a double figure-of-eight loop, but tuck the upper bight around and down through the knot as shown (fig. 1). Adjust all three loops to their required sizes and then work everything snug and tight (fig. 2).

HISTORY
The triple figure-of-eight loop was first described by Canadian climber Robert Chisnall[IGKT] in the mid-1980s.

1

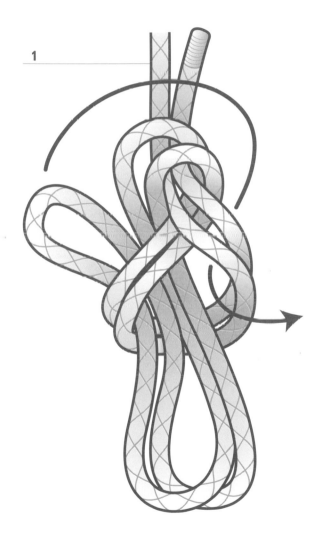

2

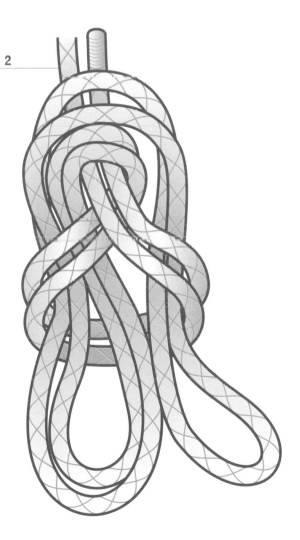

<77>

SCAFFOLD KNOT

APPLICATIONS

Make what some sailors call a 'hard eye' with this tough noose knot. It creates a sliding (adjustable) loop that is reinforced by means of a plastic or stainless steel thimble. Practised fingers can tie a scaffold knot (with thimble) in seconds, and it becomes even tighter under load.

METHOD 1 – TIED IN THE BIGHT

Create what is in effect a running (sliding) double overhand knot, as shown (figs 1–4).

HISTORY

The scaffold knot was described in Denis Diderot's *Encyclopédie* (1762).

1

2

3

4

<78>

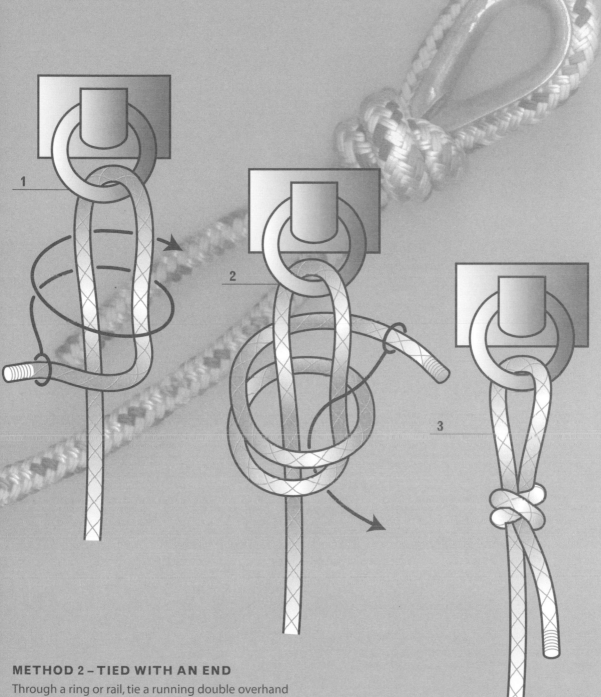

METHOD 2 – TIED WITH AN END

Through a ring or rail, tie a running double overhand
knot as shown (figs 1–3).

<79>

BENDS

Like good friends, all these knots have their quirks but ... are utterly reliable.

Frank Rosenow[IGKT], *Seagoing Knots* (1990)

Bends are joining knots, usually made in two ropes or cords of similar size and construction. A few bends are designed to cope with greatly dissimilar lines – such as when a light heaving line must be attached as a 'messenger' to precede a heavier mooring or rigging rope, which is then pulled into position – and these can also be used for any unmatched pair of ropes. Bends are also employed to unite both ends of the same piece of rope or cord, so as to create a tough, endless strop or sling for cargo handling. Never use a binding knot (such as the reef knot) as a bend; it would be unreliable and potentially hazardous to do so.

<82>

FISHERMAN'S KNOT

APPLICATIONS

Use this knot to join twines and cords of equal diameter and similar construction, when lengthening lashings or to make carrying handles (for the jug, jar or bottle sling).

METHOD

Place the two lines together, working ends pointing in opposite directions, and tie an overhand knot in each around the adjacent standing part (fig. 1). Tighten both knots and pull them together (figs 2–3). The knot has a tendency to jam in rope, but the fact that the twin knots can be pulled apart makes untying less difficult than it would otherwise be.

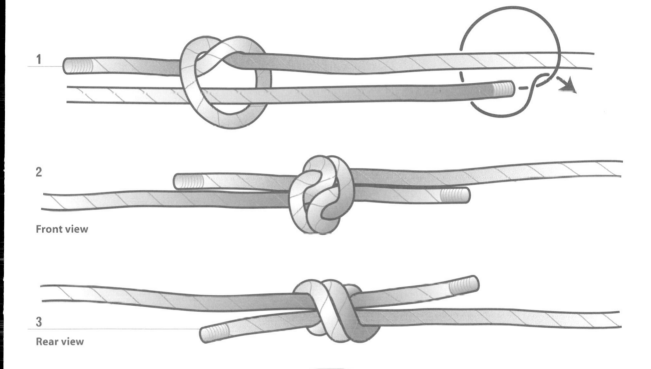

1

2
Front view

3
Rear view

HISTORY

Anglers have known this knot since at least the early 19th century by a variety of names – angler's knot, English knot, true lover's knot and water (or waterman's) knot. Captain Marryat in his novel *Peter Simple* (1834) had the character Mr Chucks, the boatswain, say of it: '... there is a moral in that knot ... that points out the necessity of pulling together when we wish to hold on.'

<83>

DOUBLE FISHERMAN'S KNOT

APPLICATIONS

In wet or slippery twines and cords, try this bulkier version of a fisherman's knot. Used in rope, it may prove impossible to untie again. I once used it to make an endless rope strop in 4in-circumference (5.7cm-diameter) manila rope, which was then used to lift the stern of a motor boat – weighing 3 tonnes – out of the water by crane to work on a foul screw; and, afterwards, I had to cut the knot off with an axe!

METHOD

Lay out the lines to be joined as for a basic fisherman's knot, but tie a double overhand knot in each end (fig. 1). Tighten both knots and pull them together (figs 2–3).

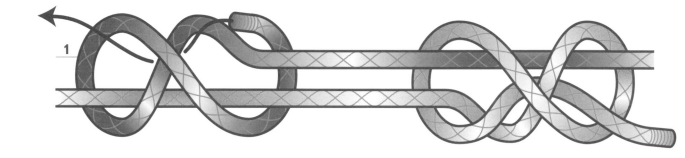

1

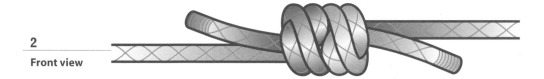

2
Front view

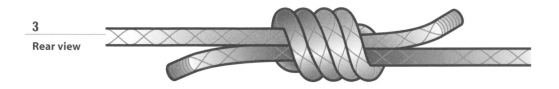

3
Rear view

<84>

SLIDING FIGURES-OF-EIGHT BEND

APPLICATIONS

This knot can be pulled apart and untied more easily than a fisherman's knot.

METHOD

Marry the two lines, working ends pointing in opposite directions, and tie a matching pair of figure-of-eight knots (fig. 1). Tighten them and then pull on both standing parts to slide the knots until they bed firmly together (fig. 2).

1

2

<85>

FIGURE-OF-EIGHT BEND

APPLICATIONS

This is a comparatively strong and secure knot for ropes of similar size and construction, less liable to jam and – with its gentle curves – kinder to the lines in which it is tied than (say) the fisherman's knot.

METHOD

Tie a figure-of-eight in the end of one rope or cord, and then introduce the working end of another line (fig. 1). Follow the lead of the original knot exactly as shown (figs 2–3) to double the knot (fig. 4). The doubled lead should cross over as it curves, and not resemble parallel train tracks. Work and pull the knot snug, compact and tight (fig. 5). Observe how the standing part of each line – upon which the load will be placed – forms the outer bight at each end of the knot. Some climbing authorities say it is stronger that way.

HISTORY

The older sea-going name for this knot was the Flemish bend. Clifford W. Ashley wrote in 1944 that it was 'bulky and bothersome to tie'. He preferred the water knot. But a consensus within the Surrey branch of the International Guild of Knot Tyers not only included the figure-of-eight knot as one of their 'Surrey Six', but urged that (as stopper, loop, hitch and bend) it ought to be the first knot taught for use in modern ropes.

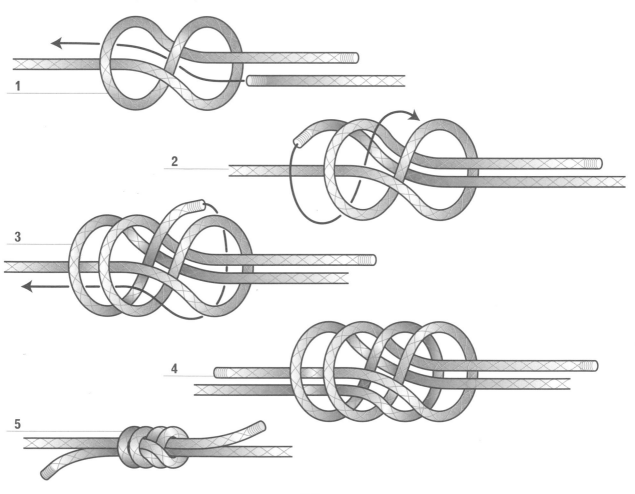

<86>

CARRICK BEND

APPLICATIONS

This is arguably the best bend for joining large hawsers and cables of more or less the same size and construction (for example, adding an extra length to a tow line, anchor rope or kedge warp). Although the knot itself – a classic – is only about 65 per cent efficient, the enormous breaking strengths of the big ropes in which it is usually tied have given it the reputation of being a heavy-duty knot.

METHOD

Make a loop in one line and lay the other on top of it, interweaving the working end under/over/under/over/ under as shown (fig. 1). The short ends should emerge on opposite sides of the knot (fig. 2), as it is believed to be more secure that way. Pull steadily upon both standing parts, to capsize the knot deliberately, until it rearranges itself into its correct loaded form (fig. 3).

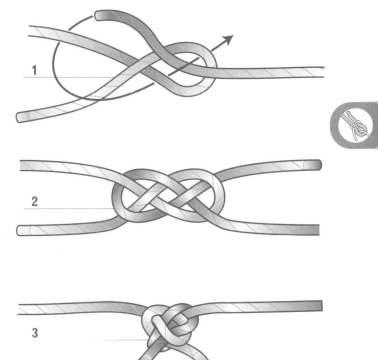

1

2

3

HISTORY

The flat symmetrical layout of this knot – with its eight crossing points – yields several possible outcomes, depending upon the over/under sequence used. The sheet bend is one, but several less reliable knots have also been misleadingly labelled as carrick bends. The true (full or double) carrick bend described above was named by M. Lescallier in *Vocabulaire des Termes de Marine* (1783) and featured by Felix Reisenberg in *Seamanship for the Merchant Service* (1922). But the origins of this knot – although uncertain – are much older. At Carrick-on-Suir in Ireland the 16th-century Elizabethan plasterwork of Ormonde Castle is embellished with numerous carrick bends moulded in relief; and a 'carrack' was a type of medieval European trading ship, from which perhaps came the Carrick Roads (a sheltered offshore anchorage or roadstead for ships) outside Falmouth Harbour, off England's Cornish coast. Then again, a carrick bend (with short ends on the same side) was the heraldic badge of Hereward the Wake, the English leader who in AD 1070 rebelled against the Normans from his stronghold in the Isle of Ely.

<87>

ZEPPELIN BEND

APPLICATIONS

This knot is ideal for attaching a boat's painter to a docking line picked up from the quayside or pier, a buoy or another boat. It will also replace a carrick bend to join towing lines or other heavy-duty ropes, coping with both unremitting heavy loads and intermittent tugging; yet it can be prised apart again with strong fingers (aided by a shrewdly directed poke or two from a fid).

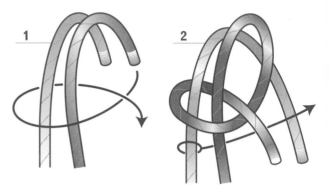

METHOD

Hold the two lines close together and half-hitch the nearest working end around both standing parts (fig. 1). Bring the standing part of the unused line forward (fig. 2), wrapping and tucking its working end as shown (fig. 3). This is one of the best of an entire family of knots that consist of two interlocked overhand knots (fig. 4). Pull it snug and fairly tight before use (fig. 5).

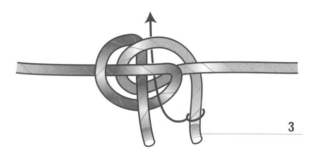

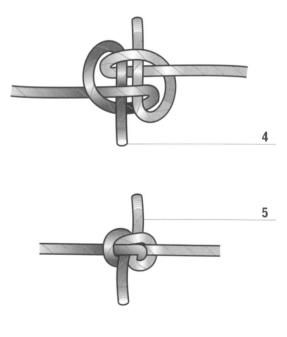

HISTORY

An article by Lee and Bob Payne called 'The Forgotten Zeppelin Knot' in *Boating Magazine* (March 1976) revealed how this knot was used until 1962 by the US Navy to tether its lighter-than-air ships. Able seaman Joe Collins, a marlinespike seamanship instructor in the 1930s, told the Paynes that he had served under the American aeronaut hero Lieutenant Commander Charles Rosendahl, skipper of the dirigible *Los Angeles*, and: 'There was only one knot he allowed ... either for bending lines together on the airship or for use on the mooring lines. I called it the Rosendahl bend.'

<88>

VICE VERSA

APPLICATIONS

Join the most slimy, slippery or otherwise intractable materials, such as wet rawhide thongs, shiny synthetics or shock elastics (bungee cords), with this bend.

METHOD

Marry the two lines, end for end, then tuck, turn and interweave as shown (figs 1–4). Pull snug and tight (fig. 5).

HISTORY

This is another knot from the inventive fingers of the late Dr Harry Asher[IGKT], who first described it in *A New System of Knotting* (1986). It may, however, have a much earlier origin. When writer and traveller Tim Severin began to stitch together his 1970s replica of the cow-hide boat used by Irish monk St Brendan in the 6th century, it took a lot of twisting and interlacing before he made something that held the wet leather thongs. He later wrote in a 1978 issue of the *Sunday Times Magazine*: '... in a curious way [the knot] looked much like the braided patterns found in Irish manuscript illustrations.' Perhaps the seafaring St Brendan used this very knot.

1

2

3

4

5

<89>

BECKET HITCH AND SHEET BEND

APPLICATIONS

When this knot is used to secure a line to a seized or spliced eye or similar permanently closed loop it is known as a becket hitch. Used to join one line to a bight in another, it is a sheet bend. There is a subtle difference in the dynamics of the two forms: in the becket hitch, any load is imposed equally upon both legs of the loop, whereas in the sheet bend, only one is loaded. The sheet bend is preferable to the carrick bend in less stiff lines, with moderate loads. It can also cope with two lines that have somewhat different diameters or dissimilar constructions, in which case the stiffer or thicker line should be used for the bight through and around which the thinner of the two is then tied.

METHOD

To make a becket hitch, pass the working end up through the loop or eye (fig. 1) and then around to lie trapped beneath its own standing part (fig. 2). When tying a sheet bend, both short ends should emerge on the same side of the knot (fig. 3), as there is some evidence that the knot may be more secure that way. For quick-release, a draw-loop may be incorporated (fig. 4).

In wet or slippery ropes, and if the bight is stiff (with a tendency to open and spill the knot), add extra security with an extra turn in tying (figs 5–6). This is a double sheet bend.

<90>

HISTORY

The sheet bend acquired its name
when it was used in the running rigging
(sheets) that was attached to sails. David Steel called it
so in *Elements and Practice of Rigging and Seamanship*
(1794). Several serious knot practitioners campaign against
using the sheet bend in lines of dissimilar size or construction,
arguing that it is safer to restrict it to being a basic bend, rather than
take the risk of having it capsize and spill from ill-judged use in mis-
matched ropes. While understandable, this is an extreme point of view,
since a useful characteristic of the sheet bend is that it will cope with
different lines. To relegate it to a lesser role is – in my judgement – to
waste this useful application of the bend. The three-way sheet bend
was spotted by Swedish yachting writer Frank Rosenow[IGKT] while in
Greek waters and berthed (docked) at the town quay in Gaios on
Antipaxos. In his book *Seagoing Knots* (1990) he credits it to
the (pseudonymous?) English colonel Bertram Bloomer,
Royal Engineers (retired). The basic sheet bend is yet
another of the six knots that the IGKT's Surrey
branch chose to recommend for use in
modern ropes.

7

8

The sheet bend may be streamlined, to
minimize the chance of it snagging on an obstacle
when pulled along, by tucking the working end back
alongside the two standing parts of the bight (figs
7–8). Then it is known as a one-way sheet bend. The
double sheet bend may be similarly modified (not
illustrated).

Three converging ropes can be joined by
means of a three-way sheet bend (fig. 9).

9

<91>

HEAVING LINE BEND

APPLICATIONS

To pass a hawser or cable from boat to boat, boat to shore, or over and across any intervening distance or barrier, first throw or convey a light heaving line (as a 'messenger') to which that rope is attached. For trivial or routine situations, this simple knot will do.

METHOD

Make a bight in the larger line and interlace the lighter one as shown (figs 1–2). Be sure to take the first turn around the longer standing part of the bight, since this will distort the knot less when it is pulled. Work the arrangement snug and secure (fig. 3).

HISTORY

Hjalmar Öhrvall included this knot in *Om Knutar* (1916).

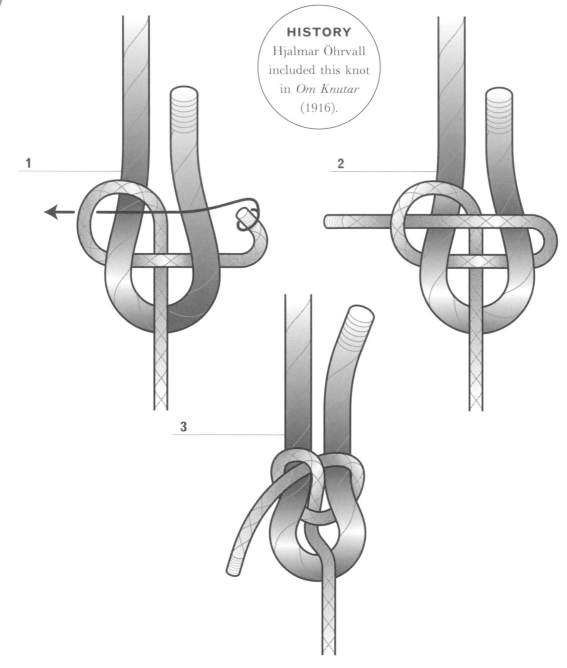

RACKING BEND

APPLICATIONS

To join a light messenger line to a much stiffer or thicker rope, use the racking bend. Racking is the term given to the figure-of-eight turns that combine to hold the bight together, preventing it from capsizing and spilling the knot.

METHOD

Make a long bight in the larger rope and tuck the lighter line so that the initial turn goes around the long standing leg of the bight (as this will distort the knot less when it is loaded). Make as many figure-of-eight racking turns as necessary to secure the bight and then tuck the working end beneath the penultimate turn (figs 1–2).

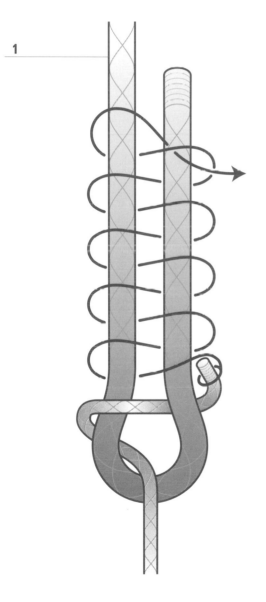

1

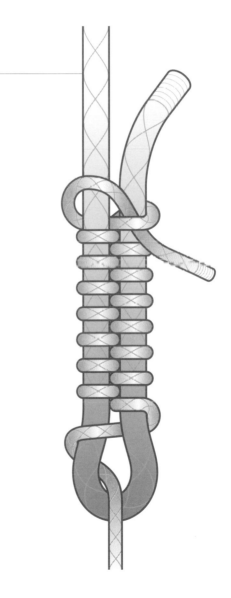

2

<93>

SEIZING BEND

APPLICATIONS
This is a heavy-duty heaving-line bend.

METHOD
Form a bight in the bigger of the two lines and then take a turn around it with the thinner line as shown (fig. 1). Begin to bind the working end of the light line neatly around both legs of the bight and itself (fig. 2), ensuring that each succeeding turn lies snugly alongside the previous one (fig. 3). Continue until near the end of the bight. Then pull the initial round turn of the light line out into a loop and place it between the standing part of the bight and its short end (fig. 4). Tighten the whole arrangement by pulling in turn upon both standing parts. For ultra-crucial situations, consider knotting or seizing the working end of the messenger line to its own standing part (fig. 5).

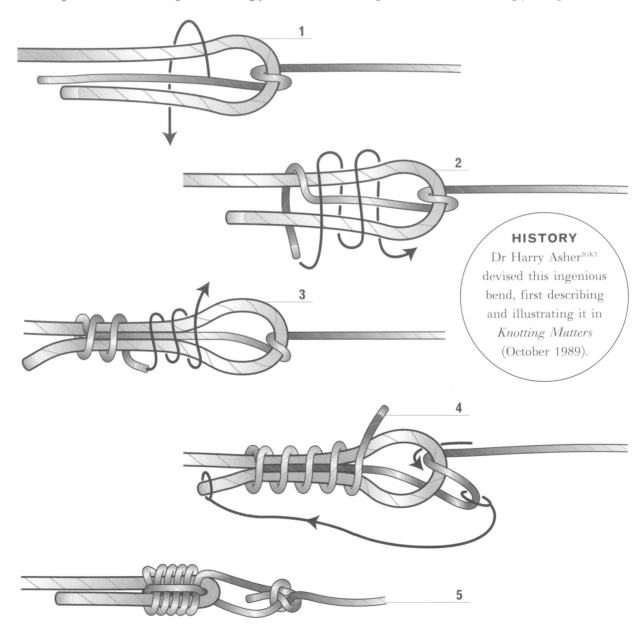

HISTORY
Dr Harry Asher[IGKT] devised this ingenious bend, first describing and illustrating it in *Knotting Matters* (October 1989).

INTERLOCKED LOOPS

APPLICATIONS

Towing lines, mooring lines and heaving lines may be joined together for extra length by the simple expedient of interlinking two loops.

METHOD 1 – BASIC

Simply tie two interlocked bowlines or other secure loop knots (angler's loops, figure-of-eight loops – not illustrated). The sharp elbows created where the two loops join may, however, prove a weak point where abrasive friction is involved.

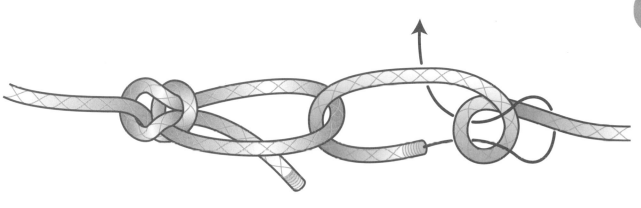

METHOD 2 – TWIN BOWLINE BEND

Marry the two ropes, working ends pointing in opposite directions, forming a loop in one standing part and tucking the other working end into a bowline layout. Repeat with the other end. Adjust both legs of the knot so that the strain falls equally upon them. Consider knotting or seizing each end to the adjacent standing part.

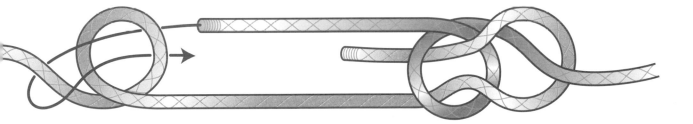

METHOD 3 – DIRECT

Partially tuck one existing loop through another (fig. 1), then pull the standing end of the second loop completely through the first one (figs 2–3). The outcome resembles a reef (or square) knot but may be somewhat stronger and is assuredly more secure. It will cope with lines of slightly different sizes and constructions.

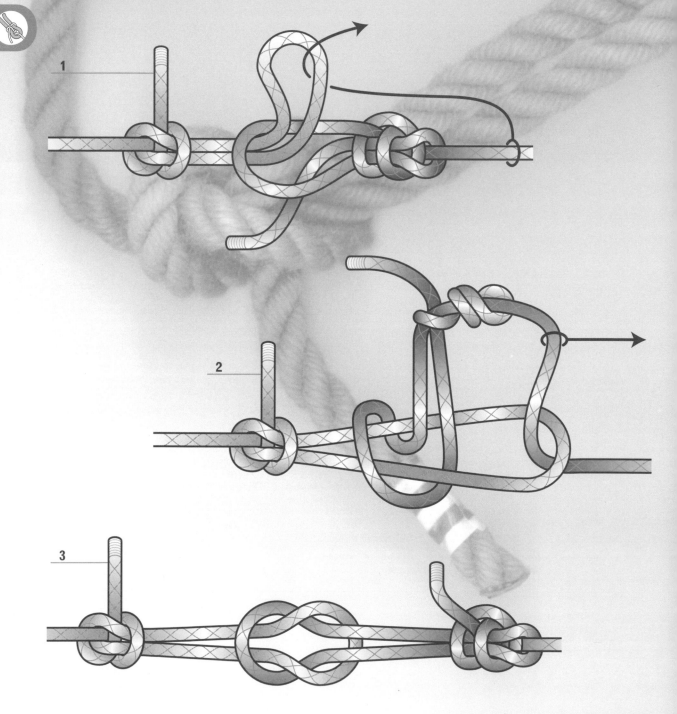

<96>

METHOD 4 – INDIRECT

The flat knot that results from method 2 (above) does not flex easily in all directions; so, given the opportunity, adopt this different approach. Tie the knot shown (figs 1–3), which is another form of the carrick bend – known as a single carrick bend, in contrast to that described earlier which, strictly speaking, is the full or double carrick bend. This knot is as flexible as a couple of chain links or a universal joint – but never use it unless each end is knotted or seized to its own standing part, as in this example. It will cope with lines that differ considerably in size and construction.

1

2

3

<97>

HITCHES

The first and forgotten genius who cast a bowline, or any one of the bends or hitches in a rope, must rank with the producers of fire through friction.

Felix Reisenberg, nautical writer (1935)

Hitches attach ropes and cords to rings, rails, spars, or even to another rope, in such a way as to withstand a load. They also belay to cleat, post or bollard, Samson post and any other solid items of hardware. As the pull may be steady or intermittent, at right-angles to the point of attachment or of varying direction and weight, no one hitch will suffice for all of these disparate requirements.

MARLINESPIKE HITCH

APPLICATIONS

Because it only exists when held together by a marlinespike, fid or other implement (such as a screwdriver), this is the most insubstantial of hitches. Nevertheless it is a hard-working one, used to improvise a handle with which extra force can be applied when tightening a knot or seizing that has been tied in any small cord or twine.

METHOD

Make an overhand loop (that is, one in which the working end is laid over the standing part of the line)(fig. 1). Bring the standing part over in front of the loop (fig. 2) and then insert the makeshift handle (fig. 3). Carefully arrange the hitch into a snug fit around the inserted tool before placing any strain upon it.

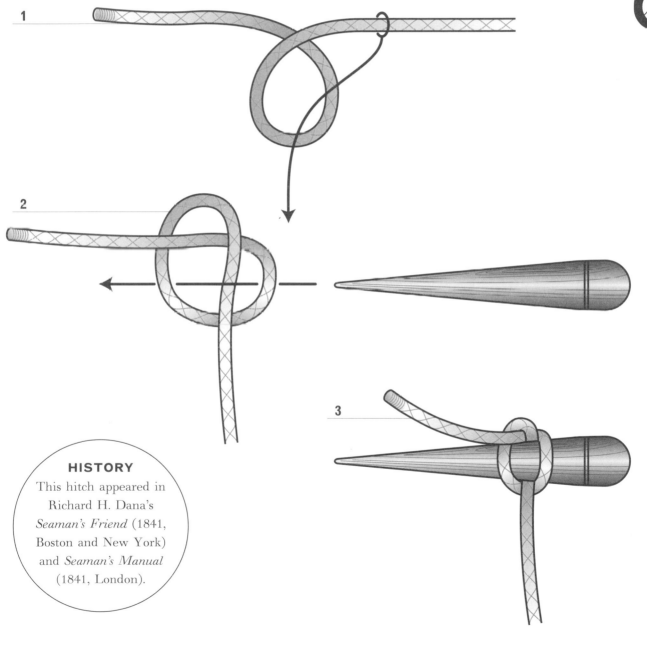

1

2

3

HISTORY

This hitch appeared in Richard H. Dana's *Seaman's Friend* (1841, Boston and New York) and *Seaman's Manual* (1841, London).

<101>

KNUTE HITCH

APPLICATIONS

Slightly more substantial than the preceding hitch, this attaches a line to anything with a hole in it that (for obvious reasons) is not much larger than twice the diameter of the cordage used. It is employed to affix lanyards to knives and other tools, while one large sailing school uses it to fasten halyards to dinghy sails, no doubt saving the cost of shackles lost overboard from inexperienced fingers.

METHOD

Tie a stopper knot in the end of the lanyard and then pass a bight through the hole in the tool or other implement to be secured (fig. 1). Tuck and trap the end (fig. 2). A bead may replace the stopper knot. By making this hitch around your belt (fig. 3) the standing end of a heaving line can be kept from following the monkey's fist on its flight through the air.

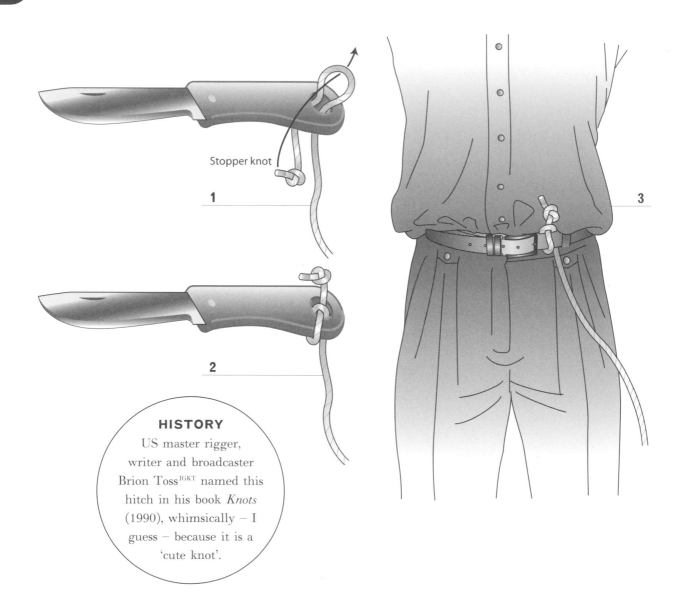

Stopper knot

1

2

3

HISTORY

US master rigger, writer and broadcaster Brion Toss[IGKT] named this hitch in his book *Knots* (1990), whimsically – I guess – because it is a 'cute knot'.

<102>

PILE HITCH

APPLICATIONS

Single fixed-loop knots are often dropped over posts or bollards and Samson posts to act as mooring hitches. The pile hitch provides a little more friction for those loops, and is also quickly tied with a bight of line.

METHOD

Wrap the loop or bight, taking it beneath the standing parts, as shown (fig. 1). Place it over the post or whatever (fig. 2) and pull it snug (fig. 3).

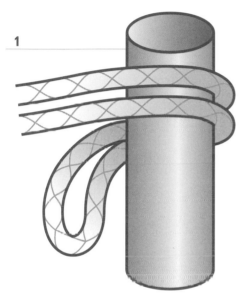

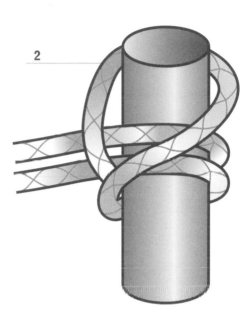

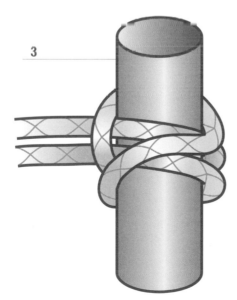

<103>

CLOVE HITCH

APPLICATIONS

This is a seasoned veteran of the waterfront, generally found working as a lightweight mooring hitch or to suspend boat fenders from a handrail. The load or pull upon it must be fairly steady and from a constant direction.

1

METHOD 1 – TIED WITH AN END

Take a turn around the ring or rail and lay the working end diagonally up and across the standing part (fig. 1). Take another turn and tuck the end beneath the diagonal, creating a letter 'N' outline (fig. 2) – or its mirror image (not illustrated). To suspend a fender or a coil of rope, incorporate a draw-loop (fig. 3).

2

3

HISTORY

Landlubbers once knew this hitch as a builder's knot. It was William Falconer who seems to have promoted the name clove hitch in his *Universal Dictionary of the Marine* (1769). It was the knot used aboard square-rigged sailing ships to fasten ratlines to shrouds, making those rope ladders up which sailormen scrambled to man the yardarms. In that splendid piratical yarn *Treasure Island* (1883), Scottish novelist and poet Robert Louis Stevenson wrote for the poor mad castaway Ben Gunn these words: 'You're a good lad, Jim ... and you're all of a clove hitch, ain't you?'

<104>

METHOD 2 – TIED IN THE BIGHT

Make an overhand loop (fig. 1), followed by another alongside the first (fig. 2). Overlap the two loops as shown (fig. 3), and the resulting clove hitch is ready to place over a post or bollard.

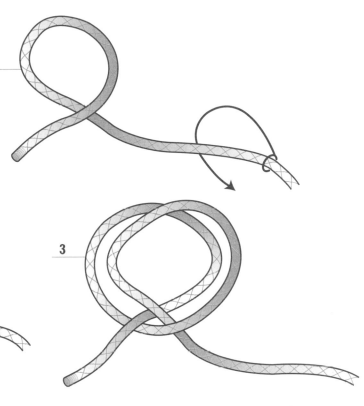

1

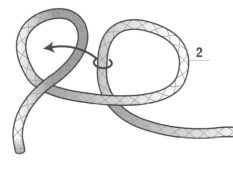

2

3

METHOD 3 – DYNAMIC

To make fast with a painter as a boat fetches alongside, cast an underhand loop (that is, one with the working end beneath the standing part) around the mooring post or bollard. If the craft still has momentum, use friction to slow and stop it. Adjust the slack to cope with any rise and fall of the berthed craft due to swells, and then add a second underhand loop over the first one (fig. 2). For all except the briefest step ashore, add other mooring lines.

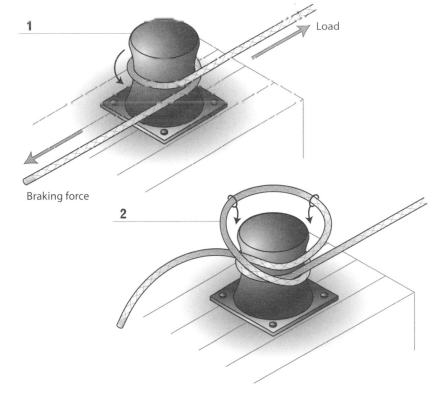

1

Load

Braking force

2

<105>

GROUND-LINE HITCH

APPLICATIONS
If the load is intermittent or varies its direction, use this holdfast as an alternative to a clove hitch.

METHOD
Begin as if to tie a clove hitch (fig. 1), but vary the final tuck (fig. 2). For an easy quick-release, use a draw-loop (fig. 3).

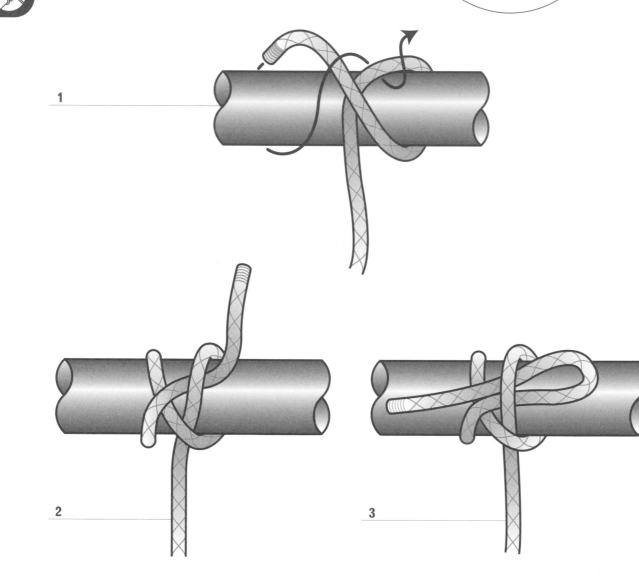

1

2

3

<106>

ROLLING HITCH

APPLICATIONS

This modified clove hitch is designed for a load or pull that comes at an angle to the point of attachment. It is an all-purpose knot that will attach to a rail the lazy painter of a dinghy lying alongside in stream or tide, and act in a flag halyard to hoist a burgee to the masthead.

METHOD

Take a turn with the working end and create a diagonal, as if tying a clove hitch (fig. 1). Wrap a second diagonal alongside the first one, between it and the standing part of the line (fig. 2). Take a final turn and add a locking tuck (fig. 3). The pull must bear upon the double diagonal.

1

2

3

HISTORY

This knot was one of the most commonly used aboard ships that relied upon rope rigging. The original, according to William Falconer's *Universal Dictionary of the Marine* (1769), was a knot that Richard H. Dana and others would later call a round turn and two half-hitches. Dana popularized its current name in his *Seaman's Friend* (1841, Boston and New York) and *Seaman's Manual* (1841, London). Other authors – Darcy Lever (*Young Sea Officer's Sheet Anchor*, 1808), George Biddlecombe (*Art of Rigging*, 1848) and David Steel (*Elements and Practice of Rigging and Seamanship*, 1794) – called it a magnus hitch or Magner's hitch.

<107>

BUNTLINE HITCH

APPLICATIONS

When a line must be tied to a becket, cringle, eye, ring or swivel that is likely to flog about in the wind, then this is the hitch for the job. It is not recommended for situations where a knot needs to be undone quickly, because it is likely to resist fingers trying to free it.

METHOD

Wrap and tuck as shown (fig. 1). The result is a cross between a running clove hitch and two half-hitches, but with the final half-hitch securely trapped inside the knot (fig. 2). Work it snug and tight against the point of attachment (fig. 3).

HISTORY

The buntline was attached to a square-sail's footrope, then passed up in front of that sail to a block on the yard, so as to pull the bottom of the sail up (brailing it) and spill the wind. As the sail would flap a lot in the process, a very secure knot was needed.

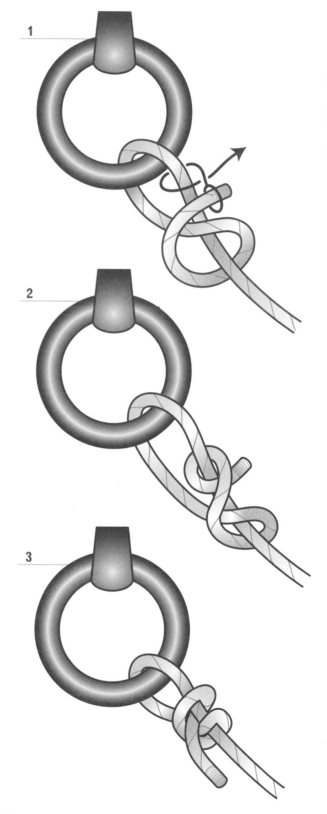

1

2

3

<108>

CAMEL HITCH

APPLICATIONS

This hitch attaches a line to mast, spars or rigging in such a way that the pull on it may be from either direction. It also undoes easily wet or dry.

METHOD

Take a couple of turns around the rope, rail or whatever, and then bring the working end across in front of the standing part and half-hitch it as shown (fig. 1). Make a second identical half-hitch (completing a clove hitch) (fig.2) and work the completed hitch snug and tight (fig. 3).

HISTORY

Clifford W. Ashley saw this knot used to tether animals to a picket line in Ringling Brothers' circus. He was told that the hitch was continually slobbered over by camels, yet could still be untied when soaking wet.

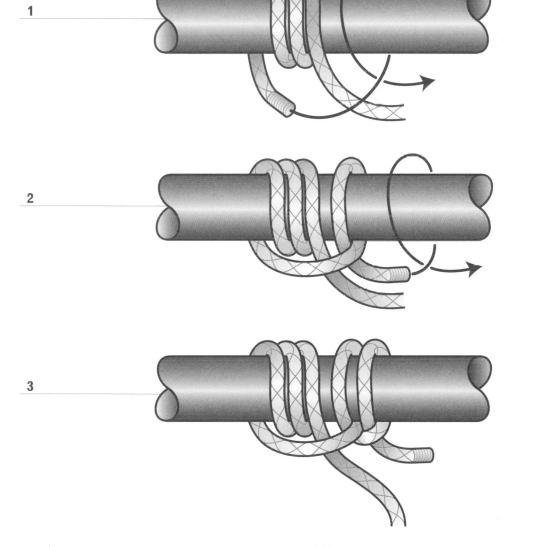

1

2

3

<109>

BOOM HITCH

APPLICATIONS

When a clove hitch, ground line hitch, rolling hitch or even a camel hitch is not considered adequate, this tough hitch will do the job. If all else fails, it really can attach the main sheet tackle to a boom – on a dinghy at least (I have done it) – and then withstand a hard beat into wind and tide to reach the causeway where car and trailer are parked.

METHOD

Begin as if to tie a clove hitch or ground-line hitch (fig. 1), but take the working end around again – first to the right, then to the left, as shown (fig. 2). The repetitive wrapping sequence is: over/over/over/over, and finally tuck (fig. 3).

HISTORY

This robust and attractive hitch was described by Clifford W. Ashley in 1944.

1

2

3

<110>

ROUND TURN AND TWO HALF-HITCHES

APPLICATIONS

Use this vintage and versatile hitch for anything and everything from mooring boats to hanging up stored gear.

METHOD

Take a round turn on ring, rail or post (fig. 1), using the inherent friction to check and hold the load. Adjust the standing part of the line to the required length, then tie a half-hitch (fig. 2). Add a second half-hitch, snug beneath the first one (fig. 3).

HISTORY

This knot was first referred to by its current name in David Steel's *Elements and Practice of Rigging and Seamanship* (1794).

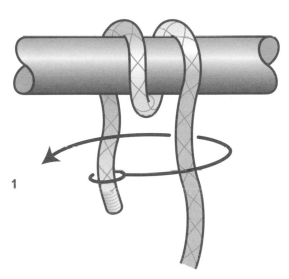

1

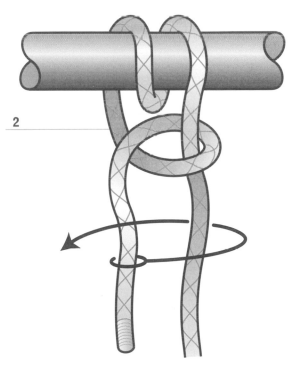

2

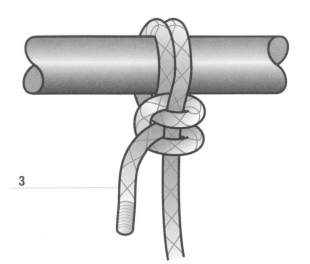

3

<111>

FISHERMAN'S BEND (ANCHOR BEND)

APPLICATIONS

This attachment is preferable to the round turn and two half-hitches when the line is a wet and slippery one, submerged (say) and covered with seaweed.

METHOD

Take a round turn and make a half-hitch through that turn (fig. 1). Add a second half-hitch (fig. 2) and pull the rope tight (fig. 3).

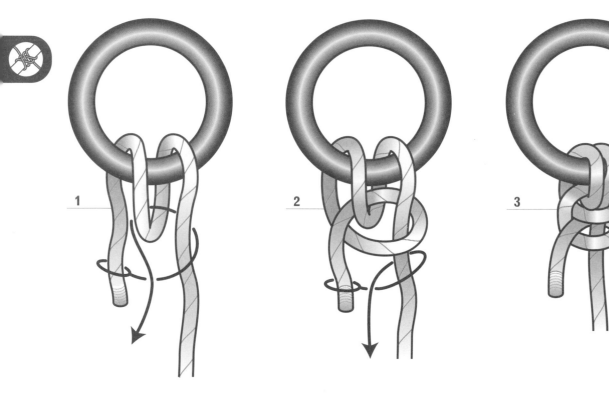

HISTORY

David Steel recommended this knot as an anchor bend in his *Elements and Practice of Rigging and Seamanship* (1794). It is because old-time sailormen talked of 'bending' a line to a ring or spar that this knot is still called a bend — when it is actually a hitch.

<112>

ANCHOR BEND (VARIANT)

APPLICATIONS

This is a compact alternative to the fisherman's bend.

METHOD

Take a round turn and make a half-hitch through it, just as for a fisherman's bend (fig. 1), but tuck the second half-hitch alongside the first one (fig. 2).

1

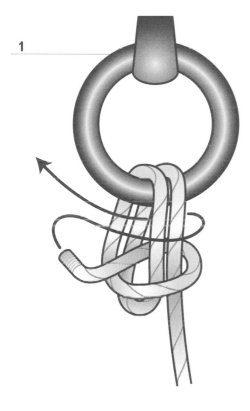

2

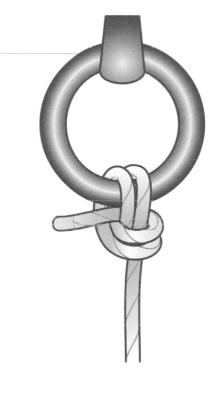

HISTORY

This neat variant appeared in the anonymous *Handbook of Sailing* (1904).

<113>

FIGURE-OF-EIGHT HITCH

APPLICATIONS

A figure-of-eight loop knot can be dropped directly over a post or bollard and used as a hitch. To tie it to a rail, however, another technique is needed.

METHOD

First tie a basic figure-of-eight knot some distance in from the working end. Then take a turn around the anchorage point and insert the working end back into the knot (fig. 1). Follow the initial lead around, in such a way that the loaded part of the line follows the outside curve (fig. 2). Work all the knot parts snug and tight.

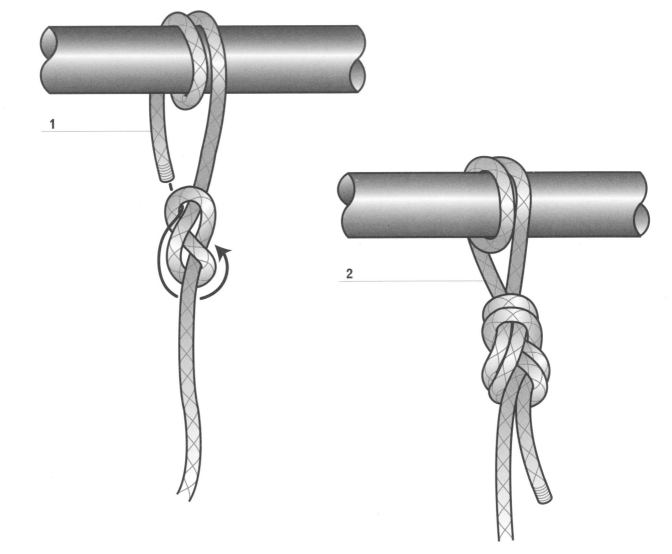

1

2

<114>

TIMBER AND KILLICK HITCHES

APPLICATIONS

The timber hitch is a quick and simple knot intended to drag, tow or hoist long objects such as tree trunks and logs, piling and piping. For smoother objects (such as masts or spars), or to give directional stability for a straighter pull, add the half-hitch that turns this knot into a killick hitch.

METHOD

Make a loop around the intended load, then tie a half-hitch and wrap the working end several times around itself (fig. 1) to create a makeshift running eye. This tucking and trapping process is known as 'dogging' the end. Pull the resulting noose tight to make a basic timber hitch. Add a half-hitch some distance from the initial knot to convert it into a killick hitch (fig. 2).

HISTORY

The timber hitch is an old knot, mentioned in *A Treatise on Rigging* (c.1625) and illustrated by Denis Diderot in his *Encyclopédie* (1762). The killick hitch was illustrated and named by David Steel in *Elements and Practice of Rigging and Seamanship* (1794), a killick being a naval term for a small anchor (or even a rock used as one); thus the killick hitch was once employed to hold any weight that anchored a boat, a buoy or even a lobster pot.

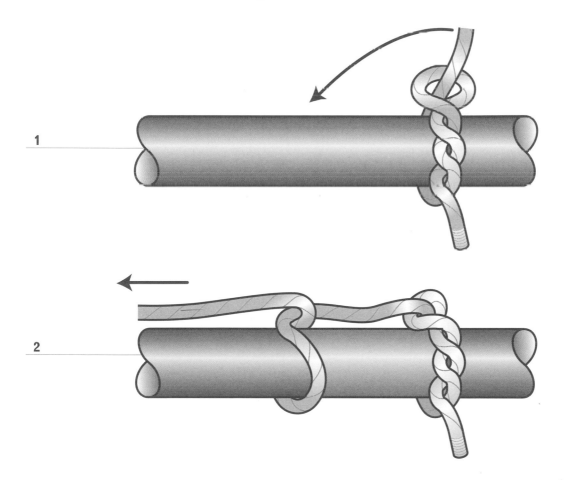

1

2

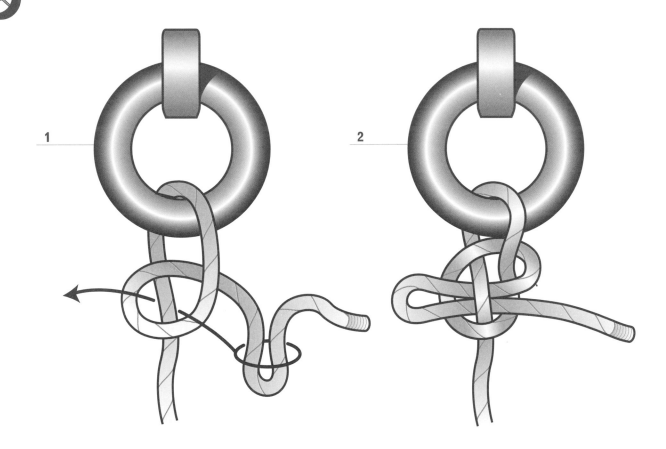

MOORING HITCH

APPLICATIONS

This is a slide-and-grip knot, with the extra convenience of a quick-release draw-loop. It will moor a dinghy or other light craft for a short time.

METHOD

Pass the line around the mooring point. Make an underhand loop and lay it atop the standing part (fig. 1). Tuck a bight over/under/over to create the draw-loop (fig. 2). Using a very long line, it is possible to bring a painter back aboard – and release it later from a distance with a smart tug; then flirt the line clear of the mooring post or bollard, and – in one continuous movement – jerk it inboard through the air (to drag it out of the water lacks flair and panache).

1

2

<116>

HIGHWAYMAN'S HITCH

APPLICATIONS

This supreme slip-knot can be used to hold almost anything that will have to be released quickly or awkwardly (with one hand, or the teeth, or from a distance).

METHOD

Tie it in the bight (figs 1–3) by inserting one draw-loop after another. The standing part will withstand a load, which a tug on the end will release (fig. 4). As with the mooring hitch, a long line may be doubled and used to release this knot from on board.

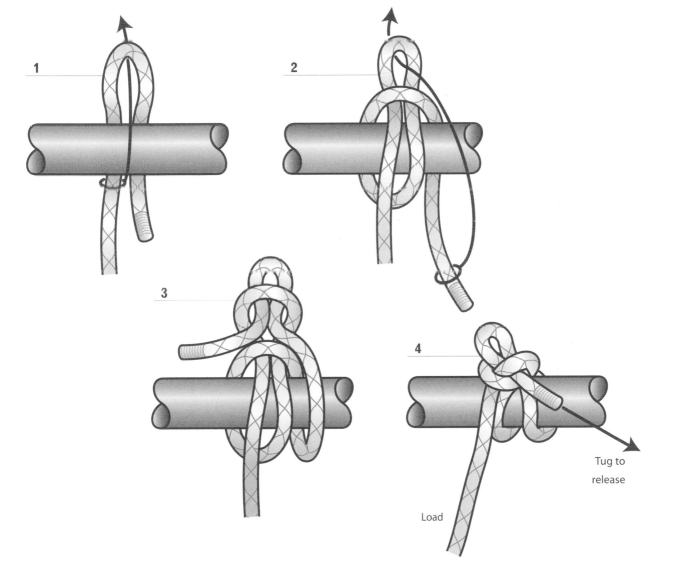

1

2

3

4

Load

Tug to release

<117>

LIGHTERMAN'S HITCH

APPLICATIONS

This is a superb hitch for rescue and salvage work, as well as routine towing. It also serves to belay a heavy-duty mooring rope or a guy-line. Whatever the load, it will hold firm, yet will not jam and can be cast off in a frantic life-saving second.

METHOD

Take a turn (fig. 1), using the friction to snub and overcome unwanted pulling power. Adjust the length of the towline or guy-line, as required, then take a bight beneath the standing part and place it over the post or bollard (figs 2–3). Finally lift the working end up, take it around the standing part and add an unsecured round turn or two on top of the existing turns (fig. 4). Do NOT finish off with a securing half-hitch or reversed loop. As the destination of a tow is approached, undo this hitch by reversing the process until only the round turn remains. Use it alone to hold the towed craft until such time as the line can be transferred to a mooring point. Alternatively, to cast off in a crisis (for example, if the tow takes a violent sheer, pulls the towing craft athwart, and threatens to capsize it), simply slide the accumulated turns upwards, off the towing post.

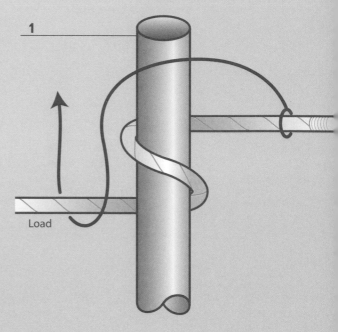

1

Load

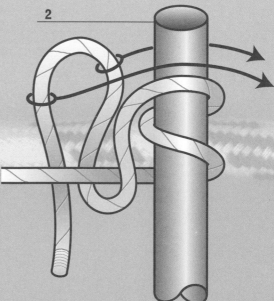

2

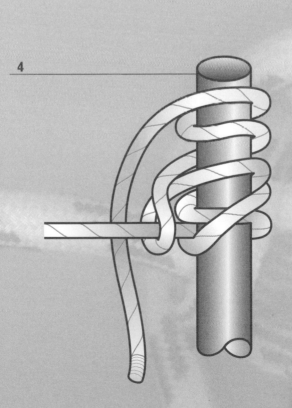

3

4

HISTORY

Seamanship manuals overlook this most practical of hitches. Riggers (in circus and theatre), as well as dockside workers, lightermen and watermen, know its worth and have used it for centuries. It has been called a boatman's hitch, while Clifford W. Ashley in the definitive *Ashley Book of Knots* (1944) referred to it as the backhanded mooring hitch. I learnt it patrolling the London river amidst tug boats and barges.

<119>

other useful knots

OTHER USEFUL KNOTS

Walking backstage at the Liverpool
Empire was like walking on the deck
of a huge land-bound sailing ship ...
the same sort of ropes, the same
knots, cleats for belaying and the
same names.

John McCarthy & Sandi Toksvig, *Island Race* **(1995)**

While a yacht or sailing dinghy may be an eye-catching,
costly purchase, it is the rigging that makes it go – and
at times all of the stresses and strains may be
momentarily concentrated upon an individual knot,
bend or hitch. These cordage holdfasts must be
shrewdly chosen to cope with the conditions in which
they will have to operate, practised until they can be
tied with your eyes shut (for sooner or later they will
have to be done in the dark), and then put to good use.
What follows is a selection of optional extras to
augment those that have already been featured.

TRUCKER'S HITCH

APPLICATIONS

This cordage contrivance tightens lashings around objects that must not shift during the voyage, such as deck cargo, dinghies, life-rafts, etc. It can also serve in a limited way, with a longer rope, as a purchase or tackle (for instance, when struggling to reach the vehicle tow-bar, with a recalcitrant trailer on a difficult causeway).

METHOD

Having made the lashing fast, bring it over the object to be secured and tie the bell-ringer's knot (an incomplete sheepshank) (fig. 1). Impart a couple of twists in the descending loop – preventing a tendency otherwise for the knot to spill – and then pull a bight

from the standing part of the line through it (fig. 2). Place this bight around a suitable anchorage point (fig. 3), levering the whole arrangement taut with the working end, prior to leading the end around a further anchorage and back across the object being secured. Repeat steps 1–3 as required.

HISTORY

The other name for this contrivance is the waggoner's hitch, which implies it is as old as carts and carriages.

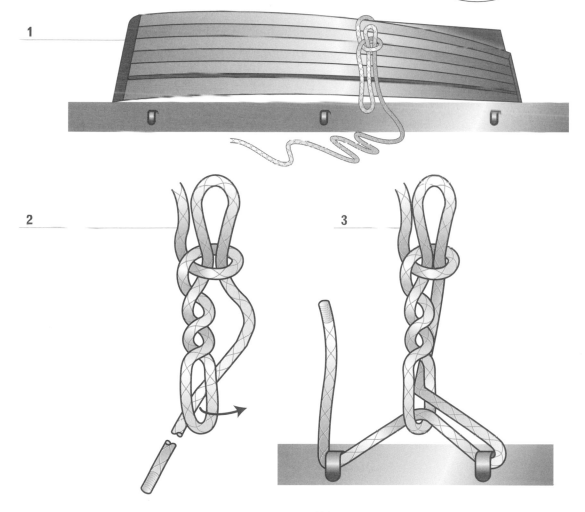

<123>

LASHINGS

APPLICATIONS

There is a continual requirement aboard yachts and other craft to lash things up (such as furled sails) or tie them down (items stowed on deck).

METHOD 1 – HALF-HITCHING

Begin with a timber hitch and then form a series of regularly spaced and evenly tensioned half-hitches around the object to be parcelled. These may be made by repeatedly pulling the long unused portion of line through every new half-hitch, but it is easier to form loops in the bight and slide each one in turn on to the parcel that is being made. Finish off with a couple of half-hitches.

METHOD 2 – MARLINE HITCHING, MARLING HITCHING

The elbows appear virtually identical, but this a different technique from the half-hitching of method 1. Marline hitching cannot be tied in the bight. Start with a simple noose, as illustrated (or a timber hitch), and tie a series of overhand knots around the foundation. The advantage is that, with clinging cord and material that grips, each knot will remain snug while the next one is tied, whereas half-hitching tends to come loose until finally secured.

<124>

METHOD 3 – CHAIN STITCH

This uses a longer lashing but looks smarter when completed. The advantage of this method is that, once the clove hitch is removed, pulling the working end will speedily undo the entire lashing like a zip fastener.

Begin with a timber hitch (fig. 1), make a series of interlocked bights (fig. 2) and finish off with a clove hitch (fig. 3).

1

2

3

<125>

INNOMIKNOT

APPLICATIONS
It is sometimes preferable to parcel with separate 'stops', rather than a continuous lashing. A series of these knots will do the job.

METHOD
Take a couple of turns with a short lashing around the object to be secured and bring both ends back to the same side (fig. 1). Make a half-hitch as shown (fig. 2). Then, with the other end, make a matching half-hitch (figs 3–4). Work snug and tight (fig. 5).

HISTORY
None to relate — except to state that this binding knot has no name. As the word for anything minus a name is 'innominate', this must be an 'innomiknot'.

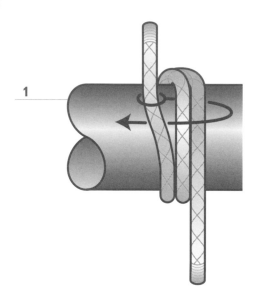

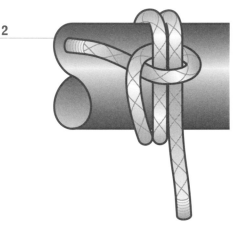

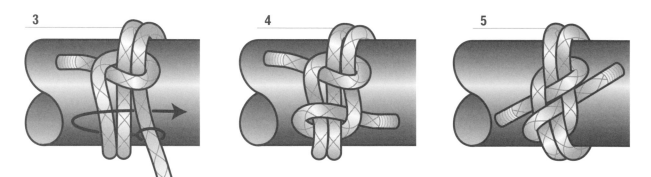

<126>

MONKEY'S FIST

APPLICATIONS

This is the knot to tie in the leading end of a heaving line – as a weight to improve its flight and distance through the air – when it is thrown from boat to shore (and vice versa), or from one craft to another.

METHOD

First make three north–south turns (fig. 1). Make a 90-degree change of direction with the working end, and enclose the first three turns with three going east–west around their equator (figs 2–3). Change direction once more, adding three final locking tucks as shown (fig. 4). Insert a large round pebble, an old golf ball or other suitable size of filler within the hollow knot, and painstakingly work the nine turns snug and tight (fig. 5). Knot or seize the working end to the standing part of the line (not illustrated).

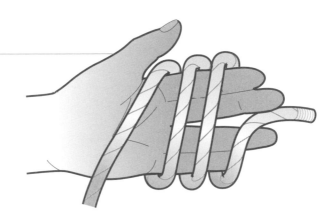

1

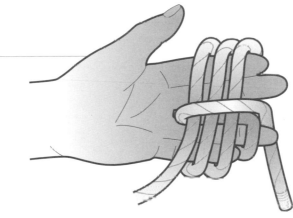

2

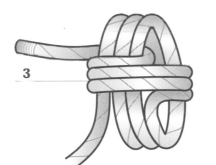

3

4

HISTORY

The monkey's fist seems to have been illustrated first by E.N. Little in *Log Book Notes* (1889). It was also described in *Sailors' Knots* (1935) by Cyrus Lawrence Day.

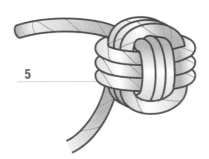

5

<127>

TWIN SPLAYED LOOPS

APPLICATIONS

Recalling the caution given earlier about the use of makeshift staging and chair knots (see Single, Double and Triple Loops), there will be times when this knot may be a better arrangement than other twin loop knots to sling and support the two legs of a ladder (or a crew member) for working over the side or aloft.

METHOD

Make a long initial bight and form two finger-like bights in it (fig. 1). Form a three-part crown knot (fig. 2). Ensure the individual knot parts lie flat and do not cross needlessly, then work the entire assembly snug and tight (fig. 3).

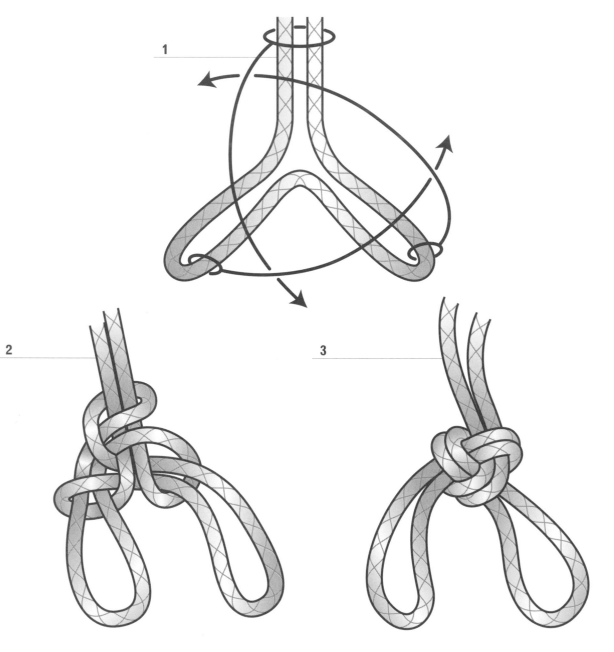

SINGLE LOOP KNOT (IN TAPE)

APPLICATIONS

Braided tape has for some years now been used increasingly in marine applications, whether for permanent docking lines or for strops to shorten mainsheet tackles and kicking straps. Tape is also ideal for lashing down canoes, kayaks and dinghies, whether on chocks atop the cabin of a boat or on a car's roof rack: being flat, there is no risk that repeated use will score grooves in what it rubs against. Woven nylon webbing and low-stretch polyester are available in widths from 10mm to 75mm (½in to 3in), but the most popular widths in use are 25–50mm (1–2in). A tubular tape, like a flattened hosepipe, ties and handles well due to its suppleness, but a flat weave (like that used for automobile seat belts) is stronger, stiffer and has better resistance to wear and abrasion. Both of these flat, strap-like materials need their own special knots, bends and hitches.

METHOD

Fold a bight (fig. 1) and simply tie an overhand knot (fig. 2). Ensure that the standing part of the tape forms the outside of the knot, which will be more secure that way.

HISTORY

While knots in straw and other flat strips may have originated in rural areas ashore, the knots featured in this section all have climbing pedigrees.

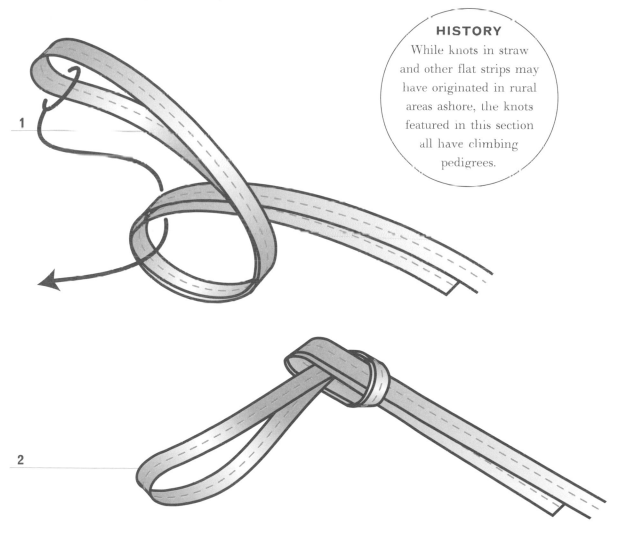

1

2

<129>

OVERHAND SHORTENING (IN TAPE)

APPLICATIONS

This is the tape alternative to a sheepshank.

METHOD

Fold an 'S' or 'Z' shape (fig. 1) and tie an overhand knot (fig. 2).

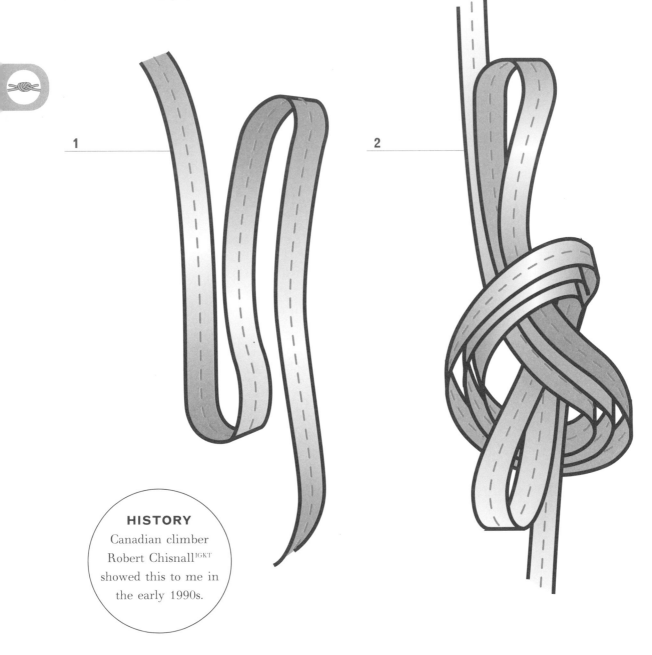

1

2

HISTORY

Canadian climber Robert Chisnall[IGKT] showed this to me in the early 1990s.

<130>

CLOVE HITCH (IN TAPE)

APPLICATIONS

This hitch actually grips better in tape than it does in rope.

METHOD

For the best possible adhesion, contrive to arrange it with the short end underneath the standing part upon which the load will fall. This is best done, if practicable, by using the long end to tie the knot (figs 1–2). Otherwise, tie it with the short working end and then rearrange it to appear as illustrated here.

1

2

<131>

TAPE KNOT (WATER KNOT)

APPLICATIONS

This is the only bend recommended by the various ruling bodies of climbing for joining two lengths of tape. It is also effective in cord, but perhaps too prone to jam to be recommended for rope.

METHOD 1 – IN TAPE (INDIRECT)

Tie an overhand knot in the end of one length of tape and introduce the other working end as shown (fig. 1). Follow the lead of the initial knot around, until it has been doubled (fig. 2). Make sure that the short ends emerge from the inside of the knot, with the long ends on the outside, as the knot is said to be more secure that way, and tighten it.

1

2

<132>

METHOD 2 – IN CORDAGE (DIRECT)

In cord it is possible to tie the knot directly (fig. 1). Once again, ensure that the long ends are located on the outside of the knot, before tightening it (fig. 2).

1

2

HISTORY

This knot is probably the 'water knot' referred to in the *Treatise of Fyshinge wyth an Angle* (1496), credited to Dame Juliana Berners (or Barnes), Prioress of Sopwell. It is certainly an angling knot from the days of horsehair and gut, appearing in Dr Hutton's *Streamcraft* (1919), as well as being an established part of the repertoire for climbers of all kinds.

<133>

EXTENDED FRENCH PRUSIK KNOT

APPLICATIONS

When shortened, this extraordinary slide-and-grip arrangement increases its diameter and so moves freely along whatever it is tied around. Stretch it, and the diameter shrinks, until it clings and will not shift. Use it to retain slack on a loaded line (for maintenance, to free a snarl-up, to cope with an emergency situation). It is also the proverbial 'sky hook' with which to suspend an overhead block, or other article, to a vertical mast or spar that lacks a fixture or fitting to hold it. And it can be used as a shock-absorber, since – by deliberately reducing the number of wrapping turns and crossover points – its holding power can be minimized so that (under an excessive load) it slides, until the energy of the falling or snatching load has been reduced by friction to a point at which the hitch will once again seize up.

METHOD

It is easier than it looks. Take eight to ten wrapping turns, criss-crossing alternately over and under (figs 1–3). Keep the 'windows' as small as possible (minimize the amount of underlying foundation that peeps through). Tie a small loop knot in each end (fig. 4) and link the two together with a shackle or a karabiner.* This is the end to which the load must be attached. To release and slide the knot, grasp the end furthest from the load and tug it so as to compress or shorten the turns.

* Karabiners make useful alternatives to shackles. With their outdoor weather-resistant finish, secure (yet easy to manipulate) gates, and safe working loads (in kiloNewtons, the SI unit of force) stamped on to their bodies, these items of hardware might have been made for boats.

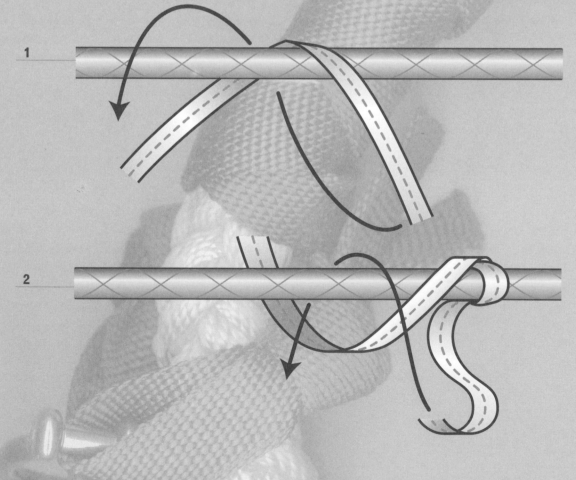

<134>

HISTORY

Prusik is the generic name for various slide-and-grip knots used in climbing, after the Austrian professor of music Dr Karl Prusik, who invented the first one during World War I for re-stringing musical instruments, and then in 1931 promoted its use as a self-rescue knot for cavers and mountaineers. The ingenious Chinese finger-trap elaboration of a prusiking hitch featured here was devised by Canadian Robert Chisnall[IGKT], who showed it to me in 1981.

3

4

Make the
loops as small
as possible

<135>

TURK'S HEAD (3 LEAD X 4 BIGHT)

APPLICATIONS

No boat should be without a Turk's head. Whether it goes on the mid-ships spoke of a yacht's wheel (to locate it by touch in the dark), or affords a slip-resistant hand-grip on a boarding ladder, a Turk's head is both practical and decorative. Advanced manuals have been written entirely about the large and diverse Turk's head family, of which this is one of the simplest but best known.

METHOD 1 – TIED FLAT

Tie a full or double carrick bend, but with the short ends emerging on the same side of the knot (figs 1–2). Tuck one end alongside the other (fig. 3) to complete

the basic knot and adjust the scallop-shaped rim parts until they are all the same size. This knot comprises 3 leads (the plaited parts) and 4 bights (the rim parts). These are its dimensions, usually abbreviated to 3L x 4B. The knot may be left flat like this, for use (say) as a thump mat to protect deck planking from a shackled block, or slid in the form of a bracelet on to a foundation (fig. 4). With one or both ends, follow the original lead around to double or triple the ply of the knot (fig. 5). A bit at a time, work all of the slack through and out of the knot, around and around, from one end of the line to the other. Repeat, using round-billed pliers if necessary, until the knot is very tight. Bury the two ends beneath the knot and cut them off flush with it.

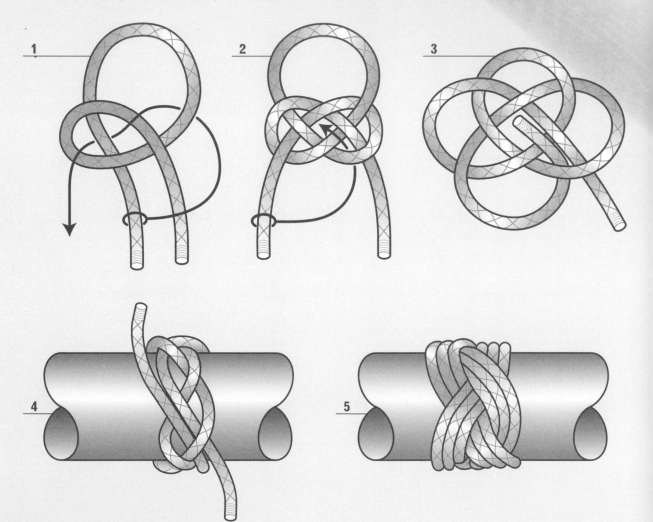

<136>

METHOD 2 – TIED IN THE ROUND

Wrap and tuck as shown (figs 1–3). Then take the working end around to rejoin the standing end (fig. 4). Spread the plaits out evenly around the foundation, double and triple the knot, then tighten. Bury and cut off the ends.

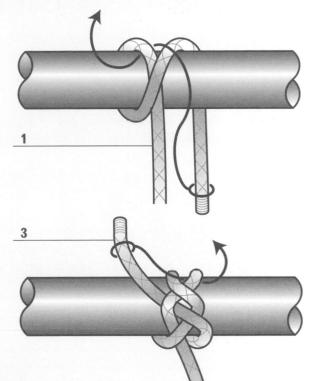

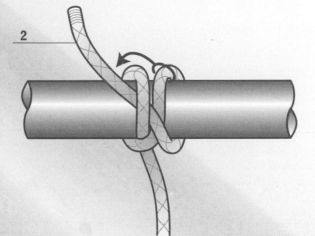

<137>

TURK'S HEAD (5 LEAD X 4 BIGHT)

APPLICATIONS

This 5L x 4B knot is a little larger than the previous one, although still what is known as a 'square' Turk's head (that is, one in which the number of leads and bights differs only by one). Use it for the same purposes – or as a handsome whipping for the ends of a rope.

METHOD

Tie it in the hand, or directly on to the knot's foundation. The initial couple of circuits (figs 1–3) create two 'ladders' along which the working end then inserts a pair of regular over/under/over locking tucks (figs 4–5). The knot may then be doubled or tripled and tightened.

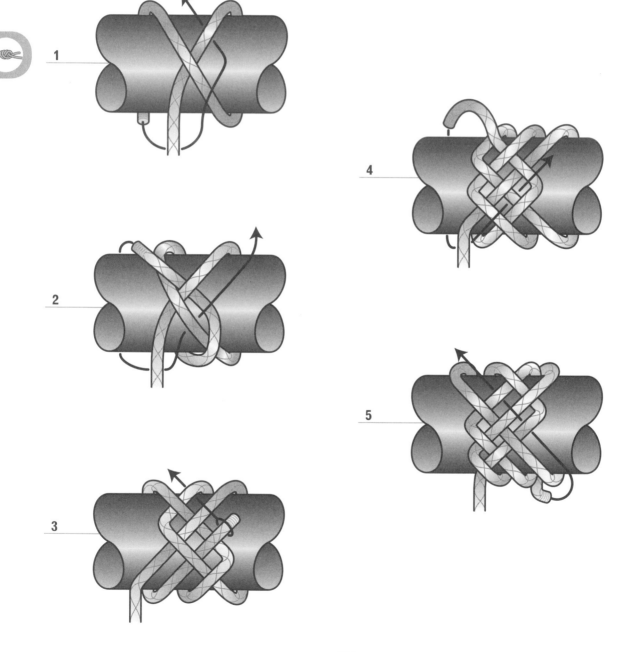

<138>

SQUARE KNOT

APPLICATIONS

This is the knot to tie in a scarf around your neck for that sortie ashore to a favourite restaurant or an exotic street market in a foreign port. The bulk of the knot nicely fills the V of an open-necked blouse or shirt, while the ends hang neatly down.

METHOD

Both ends are employed in tying the knot (figs 1–3), which must then be carefully worked snug and tight. The four-part crown (fig. 4) should be the side of the knot that shows, the distinctive cross being the rear view (fig. 5). Having learnt it like this, be prepared to adapt to tying it beneath your chin – with or without a mirror.

HISTORY

In countries such as the USA, where the reef knot may be known as a square knot, this knot has other names, including true square knot, rustler's knot and good luck knot.

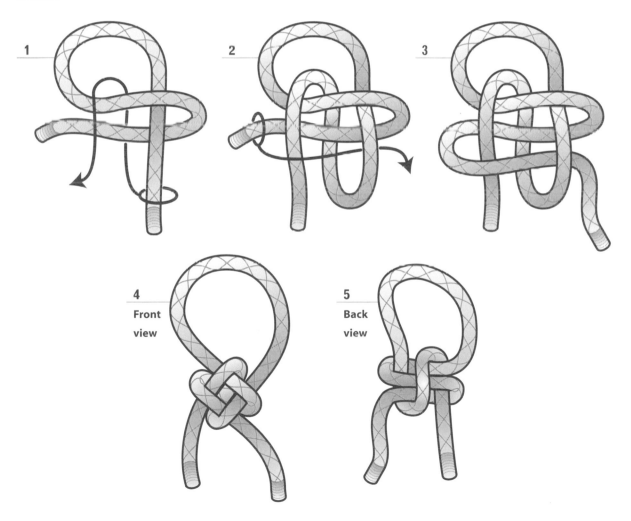

1

2

3

4 Front view

5 Back view

<139>

TEN GOLDEN RULES FOR KNOT TYERS

1. A knot, bend or hitch is either right or totally wrong; one mistaken tuck or turn results in a different knot – or no knot at all.
2. Use the simplest knot applicable to the job in hand.
3. Simplicity may be had only at the expense of friction.
4. Strength and security are distinct and discrete characteristics in a knot
5. Knots weaken rope.
6. A knot is only as good as the line in which it is tied.
7. All but the simplest of knots must be systematically worked snug, a bit at a time, prior to tightening them.
8. A poorly tied knot is less effective than the same knot properly arranged and tightened.
9. Use fingers to tie small cordage, but hands and arms to manipulate larger ropes and cables.
10. Knots that can be untied in the bight may be tied in the bight.

GLOSSARY

Becket	Loop of rope, or an eye, to which a line may be fastened
Belay	To secure a rope with 'S' or figure-of-eight turns around a belaying pin, bollard, cleat, Samson post or other solid item of hardware
Bend	Generic name for knots that join two separate ropes or other lengths of cordage
Bight	Acute bend or partial loop in a rope; also any one of the scallop-shaped rim parts of a Turk's head
Breaking strength	The manufacturer's calculation of the load that will cause a rope to fail, but taking no account of any weakening factors (see **Safe working load**)
Cable	Large rope laid up left-handed (anti-/counter-clockwise) from three hawser-laid ropes
Cord	Line under 10mm (½in) diameter (see **Small stuff**)
Cordage	Imprecise word to include every kind of rope and cord
Dog	To secure the working end of a rope by wrapping and trapping it around its own standing part
Efficiency	Strength of any knot, expressed as a percentage of the breaking strength of the rope or cord in which it is tied
Elbow	Two crossing points created close together by a loop
Eye	Small loop
Fibre	Smallest element in vegetable-rope construction, twisted to make yarns (see **Staple**)
Fray	Deliberate or accidental unlaying of a rope, causing it to unravel its component strands and yarns
Hard-laid	(Of rope and cord) Stiff due to tension applied during manufacture
Hawser	Any three-stranded rope over 10mm (½in) diameter
Hitch	Generic name for knots used to attach a line to a ring, rail, bollard, post, spar, or to another line; and to belay it to a cleat, pin, Samson post, etc.
Karabiner	D-shaped or pear-shaped metal snap-ring (a climbing accessory) with a pivoting gate that can be securely closed, and allied in use to a shackle
Knot	Generic name for all types of rope and cordage entanglements, but specifically for anything other than a bend or a hitch, namely: stopper knots, loop knots, shortenings and bindings, as well as anything tied in small stuff
Lanyard	Short length of cord used to secure an item of equipment
Lay	Direction in which rope strands and yarns spiral (right- or left-handed)

<140>

Lead	(*Say 'leed'*) Direction taken by cordage around or through an object or knot, including any over/under sequence; hence 'to follow the lead' (for example, of a Turk's head) usually means to double or triple the ply of an existing knot
Left-handed	(*Of rope*) Lay that spirals anti-/counter-clockwise as it recedes from the viewer
Line	Any rope with a particular function (such as a towline or mooring line)
Loop	Bight with a crossing point
Make fast	To secure a line to a point of attachment
Messenger	Light line used to pull a heavier working rope or cable into position
Monofilament	Long synthetic thread, the smallest element of man-made ropes
Multifilament	Bundle of fine monofilaments
Natural fibre	Raw material used in vegetable-rope construction
Nip	Point within a knot where friction is concentrated
Noose	Adjustable (running) loop knot
Part	Any inactive section of a knot; also synonymous with the word 'lead' when referring to the number of plaited strands of a Turk's head
Right-handed	(*Of rope*) Lay that spirals clockwise as it recedes from the viewer
Rope	Any line over 10mm (½in) diameter
Round turn	In which a working end completely encircles a ring, rail, post or another line, and is then brought alongside its own standing part
Safe working load	Estimated load a rope may safely withstand, taking into account its age, condition and usage (including knots); it may be as little as one-seventh of the quoted breaking strength (See **Breaking strength**)
Security	A knot's integral ability to withstand intermittent tugs, shaking, etc. (See **Strength**)
Seizing	Tight binding of thread or cord to grip and hold two ropes, or two parts of the same rope
Shackle	D-shaped, U-shaped or other metal link, closed by a threaded pin or similar device
Sheath-and-core	Synthetic cordage consisting of a braided outer sheath, containing a core of monofilaments or multifilaments that may themselves be braided, laid into strands, or a bundle of parallel yarns
Sling	Endless band or strop
Small stuff	Casual and imprecise term for any cordage (as opposed to rope)
Soft-laid	(*Of rope and cord*) Flexible due to the absence of tension in manufacture
Standing end	Opposite end of a line from the working end
Staple	Sorted and graded fibres, of limited length due to their vegetable origins
Stopper knot	Knot tied in the end of a cord or rope to prevent it fraying or escaping through a hole
Strand	Main element of rope, made in its turn from contra-twisted yarns
Strength	A knot's integral ability to withstand a load (See **Security**)
Synthetic rope	Rope and cordage of man-made monofilaments, multifilaments or film
Tape	Flat or tubular woven nylon or polyester webbing used instead of cordage for some knotting applications
Thread	Fine but strong twine (see **Twine**)
Turn	360-degree wrap around a ring, rail, post or rope
Whipping	Method of binding a rope's end to prevent it fraying
Working end	End of a rope or cord that is available for use

<141>

BIBLIOGRAPHY

There are numerous knotting manuals with a bias towards boating and sailing, although they are not always displayed on the shelves of bookshops. Current editions can be ordered and supplied in a matter of days. Some books are now out of print and may only be found in secondhand bookshops and at fairs, but a few even older classics have been revised and reissued in a modern format. The following are recommended for further reading:

Adkins, Jan, **String – Tying it Up, Tying it Down**, Charles Scribner's Sons (1992)

Ashley, Clifford W., **The Ashley Book of Knots**, Doubleday, Doran & Co. Inc. (1944); Faber & Faber Ltd (first published 1947, reprinted with amendments 1993)

Berthier, Marc P.G., **The Art of Knots**, Macdonald & Jane's (1978)

Brophy, Patrick, and Weatherston, David, **The Cockpit Book of Knots**, Tarka Press (1980)

Day, Cyrus Lawrence, **Sailors' Knots**, Dodd, Mead & Company (1935)

Jarman, Colin, **Knots in Use**, Adlard Coles Ltd (1984)

Maclean, William P., **Modern Marlinspike Seamanship**, Tree Communications Inc. (1979, 1982)

Rosenow[IGKT], Frank, **Seagoing Knots**, W.W. Norton & Company (1990)

Seidman, David, **Sailing – A Beginner's Guide**, Adlard Coles Nautical, an imprint of A. & C. Black (Publishers) Ltd (1995)

Smith, Hervey Garrett, **The Arts of the Sailor**, D. Van Nostrand Company Inc. (1953)

Smith, Hervey Garrett, **The Marlinspike Sailor**, David & Charles (1972)

Snyder, Paul and Arthur, **Handling Ropes & Lines Afloat**, Nautical Publishing Company, in association with George G. Harrap & Son Ltd (1976)

Taylor, Roger C., **Knowing the Ropes – A Sailor's Guide to Selecting, Rigging, and Handling Lines Aboard**, International Marine Publishing Company (1989)

Toss[IGKT], Brion, **The Rigger's Apprentice**, International Marine Publishing Company (1984)

Toss[IGKT], Brion, **The Rigger's Locker**, International Marine, an imprint of Tab Books, a division of McGraw-Hill Inc. (1992)

Trower[IGKT], Nola, **Knots and Ropework**, Helmsman Books, an imprint of The Crowood Press Ltd (1992)

THE INTERNATIONAL GUILD OF KNOT TYERS

The Guild was established in 1982 by 27 individuals and now has a membership exceeding 1,000 in countries from Australia to Zimbabwe. It is a UK registered educational charity and anyone interested in knots may join.

Guild members – who include many boating and sailing enthusiasts – are a friendly crowd, novice and expert alike, brought together by their common pursuit of knot tying. Those within travelling distance may enjoy two major weekend meetings held in England each year, with talks, demonstrations and expert tuition freely available, where cordage, ropeworking tools and books (new, secondhand and rare) are also bought, sold and swapped. In countries and regions where many Guild members are clustered, localized branches have formed and these arrange more frequent gatherings and activity programmes.

The thinly scattered worldwide IGKT membership keeps in touch via a handbook of members' names, addresses and other contact details, as well as a quarterly magazine, Knotting Matters, which is full of informed articles, expert tips, letters, editorial comment, news and views about everything imaginable on the knot-tying scene. The Guild also sells its own instructional publications and certain other knotting supplies by mail order.

For further details and an application form, contact:
Nigel Harding (IGKT Honorary Secretary)
16 Egles Grove
Uckfield
England
East Sussex TN22 2BY
Tel: (+44)(0)1825 760425

e-mail: igkt@nigelharding.demon.co.uk
Knotting may also be found on the Internet.

<142>

INDEX

<143>

END COMMENT

> With old sailors it was, and is, a matter of pride to be able to make knots.
>
> **Albert R. Wetjen, *Fiddlers' Green* (1941)**

Some knots are thousands of years old and, during the millennium just completed, knotted ropes have facilitated the growth and development of nations in numerous ways. They enabled entrepreneurial traders to take laden pack animals on profitable expeditions over rugged terrain, and equipped others to cross the world's oceans in search of fabled treasures and exotic new territories. Knotted ropes bucketed water up from wells, and lowered miners deep underground to probe for fuel and ores. Rope created the blocks-and-tackles that made possible the building of pyramids and ziggurats, castles and cathedrals. They also supported the canvas marquees inside which circus performers thrilled audiences with ever more daring feats on trapeze and tightrope. With knots in smaller cordage, longbows and crossbows could be victoriously strung; and church bells might be rung in dire warning or glorious celebration. Kites were flown, washing hung out to dry, and surgeons refined their suturing techniques. But it was sailors who, for a comparatively brief epoch of about 150 years (spanning the 18th and 19th centuries), enriched and endowed us with the knotting legacy we inherited from them.

By means of a length of rope and the right combination of knots, routine challenges afloat can be met and made manageable. Even a disaster might be averted. As rigger and writer Spike Africa, self-styled President of the Pacific Ocean, once declared exuberantly when an ominous wind got up, gear looked like breaking loose, and people turned to him, anxiously wondering aloud what should be done: 'Why, we'll take a reef in the roof. We'll take a turn around the cook's leg!' And readers of this book could do it.